STO
EPICUREANS AND
SCEPTICS

This study gives a comprehensive and readable account of the principal doctrines of the Stoics, Epicureans and various sceptical traditions from the death of Alexander the Great in 323 BC to about AD 200. The discussion is arranged according to topics, rather than schools, in order to bring out the underlying issues and make clear what the schools have in common and how they differ. At the same time, the coherence of each system as a whole is emphasised.

The Hellenistic philosophers and schools of philosophy have emerged from the shadow of Plato and Aristotle and are increasingly studied for their intrinsic philosophical value. Yet not only are they interesting in their own right, but they also form the intellectual background of the late Roman Republic and the early Empire. A thorough understanding of them is therefore essential for the appreciation of Latin thought and literature.

Stoics, Epicureans and Sceptics provides an introduction to the subject for all who are interested in understanding the significance of this period of ancient thought.

R. W. Sharples holds a personal Chair in Classics at University College London. He has published widely in Classical Studies and Philosophy.

STOICS, EPICUREANS AND SCEPTICS

An Introduction to Hellenistic
Philosophy

R. W. Sharples

London and New York

First published 1996
by Routledge
11 New Fetter Lane, London EC4P 4EE

Simultaneously published in the USA and Canada
by Routledge
29 West 35th Street, New York, NY 10001

Reprinted 1999

© 1996 R. W. Sharples

Phototypeset in Garamond by Intype London Limited
Printed and bound in Great Britain by
TJ International Ltd, Padstow, Cornwall

British Library Cataloguing in Publication Data
A catalogue record for this book is available from the British Library

Library of Congress Cataloguing in Publication Data
Sharples, R. W.
Stoics, Epicureans and Sceptics / R. W. Sharples.
p. cm.
Includes bibliographical references and index.
1. Philosophy, Ancient. 2. Stoics. 3. Epicurus. 4. Skeptics
(Greek philosophy) I. Title.
B505.S52 1996
180—dc20 95–26248 CIP

ISBN 0–415–11034–3 (hbk)
ISBN 0–415–11035–1 (pbk)

He who knows the limits of life knows that what removes pain due to want and renders the whole of life complete is easily obtained; so that there is no need of deeds which involve competition.

Epicurus, *Principal Doctrines* 21

Empty is the word of that philosopher by whom no affliction of men is cured. For as there is no benefit in medicine if it does not treat the diseases of the body, so with philosophy, if it does not drive out the affliction of the soul.

Epicurus fr. 54 Bailey = LS 25C

Just don't go on discussing what sort of person a good person ought to be; be one.

Marcus Aurelius, 10.16

CONTENTS

PREFACE

There are already general books on Hellenistic philosophy of several different types. This one has the following aims: to introduce the subject in a way which requires no previous knowledge either of the ancient world or of contemporary philosophy, but which will be of interest to students who already have knowledge of either or both of these; and to bring out the interest of this period of philosophical thought not only in the historical context of the ancient culture which it influenced, but also for us now. The present time is one in which the proper questioning of unthinking ethical dogmas, and the practical self-refutation of more than one ' –ism' peddled as a universal solution for all problems, may have led to a more sincere search for ethical signposts. Ancient philosophies may have something to teach us here, not indeed by way of precept but by way of illuminating – and sometimes cautionary – examples. It is in this spirit that the present introduction to *Stoics, Epicureans and Sceptics* is offered; its arrangement, by topics rather than by schools, reflects this purpose. Whether we like it or not, students of classical antiquity will bring, and always have brought, their own preoccupations and concerns along with them to their involvement with the past – consciously or unconsciously; it is better to recognise this as inevitable than to seek to deny it.

This book has grown out of two decades of teaching Hellenistic philosophy to Classics undergraduates in the University of London. In the structure of the London Classics degree as I first encountered it, 'post-Aristotelian philosophy' as it was then called (extending even then to Plotinus, rather than just to Marcus Aurelius as in some universities, but leaving the fourth, fifth and sixth centuries AD as *terra incognita* into which Classics students did not venture) was the ancient philosophy option for Latin specialists, as Greek philosophy up to and including Aristotle was for Greek specialists. Hellenistic philosophy does indeed provide an important part of the background to Roman literature, and students of that literature who want to know more about the philosophies Roman authors studied and alluded to will form an important part of the readership of this book. But not only Roman authors. Colleagues twenty years ago could still remember a time when the subject had been examined by a paper including a series of quotations from *English* literature in which candidates were asked to identify Stoic or Epicurean tendencies. It had become fashionable to ridicule such exercises; those who did so were happily unaware that familiarity with English literature of past centuries was something they were lucky to be able to take for granted, and the belittled exercise recognised that Stoic, Epicurean and indeed Sceptic ideas have come to form an important part of our own cultural background – often misunderstood or altered, but then which thoughts of earlier generations are immune to that? The hostile reaction can however only be understood in terms of the history in the twentieth century of study of this period of philosophy, of which more in Chapter One.

In accordance with the aims and intended readership of this book, annotation has been kept to a minimum. The 'Suggestions for further reading' are precisely that – they make no claim to constitute even a selective bibliography; but the items listed there in turn contain bibliographies which will help readers to pursue their studies further. One note of warning is perhaps in order here. This book is an attempt to *interpret* philosophical positions, rather than simply reporting their proponents' own words (in so far as that is possible anyway, given the state of our sources); as with any such attempt, this involves a (necessarily one-sided) debate with the ancient thinkers, bringing out the apparent implications of their actual statements and endorsing or objecting to them. The reader should thus not take everything in this book as a straightforward recording, or even an attempted reconstruction, of the Stoics', or the Epicureans', or the Sceptics' very own words. Citation of specific evidence will clarify this distinction to some extent, but neither space nor the character of the book allow full documentation and discussion of the extent to which every interpretative claim rests either on evidence or on informed speculation. Those who wish to pursue these issues further – and it is

hoped that many readers will – are urged to refer to the original
sources themselves.

This book is not intended as a source-book of translations from
the original texts; that would be superfluous given the ease with
which much of the evidence can now be consulted in Long and
Sedley, *The Hellenistic Philosophers* (see List of Abbreviations),
and I have accompanied citations of original works by references
to Long and Sedley's collection wherever appropriate. I have, however, included a considerable number of translations of original
texts, with the intention not so much of presenting the whole
range of evidence as of giving some idea of the flavour of the
original writings. To attempt to reproduce in English the grandeur
of Lucretius or the pointed rhetoric of Seneca would be a tall
order indeed; and the translations here are 'philosophers'
translations', giving priority to accurate rendering of the
arguments rather than to literary graces. Even so, the presence
of ancient voices in however barbarised a form may make the
book more readable than it would otherwise be. I have endeav-
oured where possible, both in the translations and in my own
discussions, to use gender-inclusive language, I hope not too jar-
ringly; the presuppositions of the societies which provided the
context for the theories discussed in this book sometimes make
this difficult, but it seems not inappropriate given that one of the
themes of this book is the timeless and hence contemporary rele-
vance of Hellenistic ethical thought. Moreover, both the Stoics
and the Epicureans held that both women and men could be
philosophers; see note 12 to Chapter Two and notes 4 and 9 to
Chapter Six.

All translations in this book are my own. That of Gellius
7.2.7–11 in Chapter Four is reproduced with permission from p. 99
of my *Cicero: On Fate and Boethius*: Consolation of Philosophy
IV.5–7 and V, Warminster, Aris and Phillips, 1991. It would be
impossible to name everyone who has contributed to my understanding of the subject, imperfect as it nevertheless is, but I would
like to thank the participants in ancient philosophy seminars at
the Institute of Classical Studies, University of London, and the
colleagues, postgraduates and undergraduate students with whom
I have discussed these issues in seminars and individually. The
responsibility for any misuse I have made of their thoughts or
suggestions remains, of course, my own. I would like to dedicate
this book to the memory of the colleague, Mark Gretton, with

whom I shared the teaching of the subject for ten years. Above all my thanks for support and tolerance are as ever due to my wife Grace and daughter Elizabeth.

University College London

September 1995

ABBREVIATIONS

[ ] indicate explanatory additions in the *translations*; < > translations of editorial additions to the original Greek or Latin texts.

ad Hdt.	Epicurus, *Letter to Herodotus*
ad Men.	Epicurus, *Letter to Menoeceus*
Annas	Julia Annas, *The Morality of Happiness*, New York, Oxford University Press USA, 1993
DL	Diogenes Laertius, *Lives of Eminent Philosophers*
EK	L. Edelstein and I. G. Kidd, eds, *Posidonius, The Fragments*, 2nd edn, Cambridge, Cambridge University Press, 1989
EN	Aristotle, *Nicomachean Ethics*
Galen, *PHP*	Galen, *On the Doctrines of Hippocrates and Plato (De placitis Hippocratis et Platonis)*
KRS	G. S. Kirk, J. E. Raven, M. Schofield, *The Presocratic Philosophers*, 2nd edn, Cambridge, Cambridge University Press, 1983 (References to their pages are preceded by 'pp.'; numbers not preceded by 'pp.' indicate their numbered texts)
LS	A. A. Long and D. N. Sedley, *The Hellenistic Philosophers*, Cambridge, Cambridge University Press, 1987 (References as for KRS; to the first volume unless otherwise indicated)
Nussbaum	Martha C. Nussbaum, *The Therapy of Desire: Theory and Practice in Hellenistic Ethics*, Princeton, Princeton University Press, 1994
PD	Epicurus, *Principal Doctrines*
Plutarch, *CN*	Plutarch, *On Common Notions, against the Stoics (De communibus notitiis)*

Plutarch, *SR*   Plutarch, *On Stoic Self-Contradictions* (*De Stoicorum repugnantiis*)

Sextus, *M*   Sextus Empiricus, *Against the Professors* (*Adversus mathematicos*)

Sextus, *PH*   Sextus Empiricus, *Outlines of Pyrrhonism* (*Pyrrhoneiai hypotyposeis*)

SVF   H. von Arnim, *Stoicorum Veterum Fragmenta*, Leipzig, Teubner, 1903–5

1

HELLENISTIC PHILOSOPHY
Aims, context, personalities, sources

AIMS AND CONTEXT

So now I lay aside poetry and other trifles; what is true and proper, that I care about, and ask about, and am totally involved in .... And so that you shan't ask me under what leader, and in what philosophical household, I seek protection, I have not signed up to swear an oath to any master, but come ashore as a guest wherever the storm carries me. At one moment I become active and plunge into the waves of the state, a guardian of true virtue and her unbending servant; at another moment I stealthily slip back into following the precepts of Aristippus, and try to be superior to circumstances rather than submitting to them.

(Horace, *Epistles* 1.1.10–19)

Horace is writing a poem, and we must allow for poetic licence. But his remarks may stand at the start of this discussion as a reminder – along with many other passages in Roman literature – that it was the philosophies developed in the Hellenistic period, that is to say after the death of Alexander the Great in 323 BC, that provided the intellectual context for the late Republic and early Empire. (The unbending servant of true virtue, active in the affairs of state, is Stoic; Aristippus, like Epicurus, advocated the view that pleasure is the goal of life, but in a form with which Epicurus disagreed, as we will see in Chapter Five.) Earlier Greek philosophical writings – in particular, Plato's dialogues – were both studied and influential; but even they were read in this period in the light of Hellenistic preoccupations. Cicero's philosophical writings reflect his education in Hellenistic philosophical

1

debate; Lucretius turns dry Epicurean prose treatises into moving rhetorical poetry; Seneca's prose writings explicitly, and his tragedies implicitly, draw upon Stoic philosophy – and Epicurean too. Virgil in the sixth book of the *Aeneid* constructs from Stoic and Platonic-Pythagorean materials an account of the destiny of the human soul and its place in the cosmos which suits his own patriotic purposes; the former slave Epictetus and the Roman emperor Marcus Aurelius (both indeed writing in Greek) each presents Stoic teachings in his own way.

The philosophies of the Stoa and of Epicurus provided Horace and other Romans not just with abstract philosophical doctrines or with material for literary exploitation, but with views on how life should be lived. That was the explicit concern of both schools. It is an aim that deserves to be taken seriously and will be taken seriously in this book, and that for two reasons.

First, the time is ripe to do so in terms of the progress of modern scholarship. Hellenistic philosophy, as presented in the Latin writings of (above all) Cicero and Seneca, was a staple of western European education, and thus an indirect source of practical guidance, up until the nineteenth century. Indeed in the latter part of that century presentation copies of the writings of Epictetus and Marcus Aurelius, along with Fitzgerald's version of Omar Khayyam, played among free-thinkers something of the role of gifts to the young on significant occasions that leather-bound Bibles and prayer books played among the Christian devout; and the tone of some of the older books on Stoicism, in particular, still to be found in libraries is oddly devotional to the modern ear. But the other side of the coin was that in some academic circles Hellenistic philosophy came to be seen as a period of decline; partly because of the nineteenth-century swing towards things Greek rather than things Roman, combined with assumptions about a decline of Greek culture generally in the Hellenistic period, and partly because the pre-eminence of Plato and Aristotle made it seem as if the history of Western philosophy could be studied without much reference to the Hellenistic period. Moreover, in England at least in the middle years of the twentieth century a practical concern with how people should live was not seen as a prominent part of the business of philosophy. That would indeed have seemed absurd to Plato, and even to Aristotle, departmentalised though his view of philosophy was; but, for better or worse – and as events showed, for the better – it became necessary to re-establish the credentials of Hellenistic philosophy *as philosophy* if it was to be taken seriously.

That re-establishment has been one of the major achievements of twentieth-century classical scholarship. It has become clear, for example, that Stoic logic and philosophy of language anticipated recent developments in ways that had not previously been realised, partly because of the nature and obscurity of the sources, of which more shortly, but partly because the departmentalisation of modern scholarship had driven a wedge between philology and contemporary philosophical concerns.[1]

Fortunately, the philosophical credentials of Hellenistic philosophy can now be regarded as re-established. We can thus safely restore the question 'what is the best way for people to live?' to the central position that it held for the Hellenistic schools themselves, without risking the charge that this is moralising rather than philosophy. And that charge would in any case – which brings us to the second point – be far less likely in the present-day intellectual context, where the question may seem particularly urgent. Traditional values and institutions have been rejected or weakened by self-styled modernisers of various types. Recent attempts to reduce all human activity to economic competition are being questioned. And religious or quasi-religious cults and fundamentalisms of various types hasten to fill the gap by offering answers to moral questions.

The search for values by which to live, the question of the proper place of competition in human life, and the tension between sectarian dogma and argument were indeed already issues in the period of thought we are studying. This search for values has sometimes been linked – especially by those who saw it as moralising rather than philosophy, and so as evidence of decline – to the changed political and social situation after the conquests of Alexander the Great. There is some truth in this picture, though to question traditional moral and political arrangements had already been the business of philosophy for over a century, since the Sophists in the fifth century BC. But, regardless of specific similarities between then and now, we may have something to learn from earlier thinkers, if not about how human beings in fact ought to live, at least about what sort of question that might be asked and how we might set about answering it. More than one recent writer has suggested that the ancient Greek culture that preceded philosophy proper might be worth studying in this connection;[2] and

3

the same may be true of the philosophy of the Stoics, Epicureans and Sceptics as well. At least we can learn from what we may find to be their mistakes or limitations. In a more immediate way one recent writer has told of the strength he gained, when a prisoner of war, from the writings of the Stoic Epictetus.[3]

It is perhaps *possible* to study ancient philosophical doctrines, or ancient works of literature, in a purely antiquarian way without being motivated by contemporary concerns in doing so and without letting ourselves be affected by them at all. But even if such detachment is humanly possible, which seems doubtful, it seems needlessly restrictive, provided always that we retain a sense of historical perspective and seek to be aware of differences between ourselves and the ancients as well as of similarities.

THE PARTS OF HELLENISTIC PHILOSOPHY AND THE ARRANGEMENT OF THIS BOOK

The Stoics conventionally divided philosophy into three parts: logic, or the study of reason; physics, or the study of nature and the cosmos; and ethics, or the study of human nature and how we should live. (Stoic 'logic' was wider in its scope than the modern term would suggest, including not only our logic but also, on the one hand, epistemology or the theory of knowledge, and on the other hand, the study of language and rhetoric.) This threefold division became standard in later ancient philosophy. Epicurus rejected logic in our sense of the term and indeed rhetoric too, and confined the first part to theory of knowledge or, as he called it, 'canonic' (from *kanôn*, a rule or yardstick by which we can judge the truth). There were debates within the Stoic school over the order in which the three parts should be studied; there was however general agreement that theory of knowledge came first, since unless we know how we can know anything we have no foundations on which to build. The Sceptics, denying that we *can* know anything, in a sense got no further than this first stage.

There are two ways in which a survey of Hellenistic philosophy could proceed, either by schools or by topics. In the present book the latter arrangement has been selected, for two reasons. Although the Stoic and Epicurean doctrines were in some respects diametrically opposed, they also have many features in common, and an approach by topics will serve to bring out these differences and similarities. There are ancient precedents for recognition

4

of the common property that the schools shared; Seneca, though writing as a Stoic, is ready to make use of Epicurean doctrines too where they suit his purpose:

> Let us thank God that no one can be forced to stay alive; we can trample on necessity itself. 'Epicurus said that,' you say; 'what are you doing with what belongs to someone else?' My property is – the truth. I will continue to hurl Epicurus at you, so that those people who swear oaths of loyalty and reckon not what is being said, but who said it, may realise that what is best is common property.
>
> (Seneca, *Letters on Morals* 12.10–11;
> see also Chapter Five)

An arrangement by topics will also facilitate comparison with modern preoccupations – most obviously in ethics, but not only there.

THE PERSONALITIES AND THE SOURCES

A major difficulty in the study of Hellenistic philosophy is the relative lack of primary sources. Something therefore needs to be said straight away about the nature of our evidence; and this can helpfully be combined with an introduction to the major personalities in the various schools.[4]

Epicureanism

Epicurus, born in 341 BC in Samos to a family of Athenian colonists, set up his school, the Garden, in Athens in 307/6 BC. The story is told that he was moved to study philosophy by the inability of his schoolteacher, when he came to the line in Hesiod's *Theogony* (116) 'First of all Chaos came to be', to explain to him where Chaos came from. His philosophy is a development – though with very significant modifications, as we shall see – of the doctrines of the fifth-century atomists Leucippus and Democritus, and he was taught by an atomist philosopher, Nausiphanes; according to ancient reports Epicurus disparaged his teacher and other philosophers generally, but some of these reports reflect the tendentious hostility of a member of his school who had quarrelled with him.[5] Epicurus died in 270 BC.

His writings have survived partly by manuscript transmission

and partly in papyrus fragments. Diogenes Laertius, in his popular-
ising account of *The Lives of the Philosophers* (probably written
in about 200 AD), devoted the whole of the tenth and final book
to Epicurus, and included in their entirety three letters of Epicurus
and the collection of *Principal Doctrines*. The first letter, to Herodotus (not the historian), is a summary of the whole of Epicurus'
system intended as an *aide-memoire* for those already familiar with
it; the second, to Pythocles, which may in its present form be only
a summary of the original, is concerned with astronomical and
related phenomena; the third, to Menoeceus, is concerned with
ethics. We also have a collection of sayings of Epicurus in a Vatican
gnomologium or anthology.

In addition, we possess extensive fragments of Epicurus' other
writings – and especially of his treatise *On Nature*, in thirty-seven
books – among the papyri excavated from the library of the villa
at Herculaneum, buried under liquid mud by the eruption of
Vesuvius in AD 79, of one of the family named Piso, a family
which had included the patron of the Epicurean Philodemus (p. 7).
At Pompeii red-hot ash from the same eruption destroyed all
combustible material; but the mud that engulfed Herculaneum, by
cutting off the air, ensured the preservation, in carbonised form,
of wooden objects such as furniture – and also of documents on
papyrus. Part of the library was excavated in the eighteenth
century; the remainder is still buried under what has long since
become not mud but solid rock. Needless to say, the unrolling
and reading, let alone the interpretation, of texts on carbonised
rolls of papyrus has been a slow process, not helped by the obscurity of Epicurus' prose style, and much still remains to be fully
understood even from what has already been excavated.

Epicurus asserted that words should be used in their immediate
and most obvious sense (*ad Hdt.* 38). Laudable though this aim
might be, and in accordance with the Epicurean emphasis on
clarity, Epicurus, who rejected traditional culture, failed to realise
that making one's writing attractive to the general reader can actually help in communicating one's point, and while he certainly
uses each word in a single well-defined sense he achieves this by
concocting obscure jargon which makes his writings heavy going
for the uninitiated. But then it is not clear how far Epicurus
intended his writings to appeal to those who were not already
devotees of his system; the *Letter to Herodotus* is explicitly (35)
intended for those familiar with Epicurus' teachings already, and

while it may be wrong to judge Epicurus himself by his followers'
summarising of the first four Principal Doctrines in a 'fourfold
remedy', an amulet against doubt – 'God is not to be feared, death
should cause no apprehension, and the good is easily obtained, the
terrible easily endured' (LS 25J) – Epicureanism does seem to have
about it something of the closed world of the religious sect. It was
to have distinguished adherents, including Romans active in politics in the first century BC (notably Cassius, the conspirator against
Julius Caesar); on the face of it such political involvement fits
oddly with a doctrine that advocated withdrawal from politics. It
seems that one could be influenced by Epicurean principles without necessarily adopting an Epicurean way of life altogether.[6]

The Herculaneum papyri preserve works by other Epicureans,
notably Philodemus (c.110–c.40/35 BC). Philodemus wrote distinguished Greek elegiac poetry, but explicitly rejected the use of
poetry as a medium for conveying philosophical thought. The
Latin writer Lucretius, however, in the 50s BC, gave some aspects
of Epicurean doctrine a poetic and rhetorical expression which
probably did more than anything else to ensure their survival.
Lucretius based his poem on Epicurus' writings, but replaced Epicurus' dry exposition and rebarbative jargon by vivid imagery and
emotive language. His presentation of Epicureanism is indeed par-
tial; Epicurus' general ethical teachings appear mainly in the pro-
logues to the six books of which Lucretius' poem is composed,
and the main concern of the poem is with the exposition of
Epicurean physical theory and of the first two lessons of the
Fourfold Remedy which closely depend on it, denial of the immortality of the soul and denial of the concern of the gods with human
affairs.

Diogenes Laertius' account of Epicurus, already mentioned,
includes reports of Epicurean doctrine as well as quoting writings
by Epicurus himself. There are numerous – more or less tendentious – references to Epicurus' teachings in non-Epicurean writers
such as Cicero, Seneca and Plutarch. There is also one additional
ancient Epicurean source, the oddest of all. In the second century
AD another Diogenes, a wealthy inhabitant of Oenoanda in what
is now southern Turkey, set up, for the benefit of his fellow-
townsmen, along one side of the town square, a portico containing
an inscription setting out Epicurean doctrines in his own words,
accompanied by extensive quotations from Epicurus himself.
According to the latest reconstruction[7] the inscribed area was

about 80 metres long and 3¼ metres high. The piecing together of the text from the blocks on which it was carved, now scattered on the ground, combines archaeology, knowledge of building construction, epigraphy (the study of inscriptions) and ancient philosophy in a way that few if any other branches of classical studies can claim to do.

Stoicism

The Stoic school, which took its name from its beginnings in the *Stoa poikilê* or Painted Porch, in the main square of Athens, was founded by Zeno (335–263 BC) from Citium in Cyprus; he had previously been a pupil of Polemo, the fourth head of Plato's Academy, and of the Cynic Crates. Zeno was succeeded by Cleanthes (331–232 BC) from Assos in Asia Minor, and Cleanthes by Chrysippus (c.280–207 BC), also from Cyprus; it was Chrysippus more than anyone else who developed and formulated the teachings of the school. But of the writings of these three Stoics, and indeed of Chrysippus' successors Diogenes of Babylon (c.240–152 BC) and Antipater of Tarsus (second century BC), nothing remains except a few papyrus fragments and numerous reports in later writers, some of whom are overtly hostile and tendentious, and all of whom may be influenced by their own preoccupations or simply fail to understand fully the doctrines they are reporting.

While Epicureanism remained something of a sect apart, separate from the mainstream of philosophical and intellectual debate, the Stoics engaged in continuous controversy with the sceptics of the Academy, and their philosophy was a major influence on political and ethical thought in the Roman Empire in the last century BC and the first two centuries AD. Both these factors led to changes, at least of emphasis; and Stoic philosophical agendas and Stoic philosophical jargon had great influence even among those who did not accept all the tenets of the school. Panaetius of Rhodes (c.185–109 BC) was an associate of the Roman statesman Scipio Aemilianus, the conqueror of Carthage; as we shall see, Panaetius modified the emphasis of the school's teachings in such a way as to make them more directly relevant to the practical concerns of real people. His writings were a major source for Cicero's *On Duties*. Posidonius of Apamea in Syria (c.135–c.50 BC) also modified the traditional doctrine of the school, especially in psychology, but his main interest seems to have been in specific

8

sciences such as geography and ethnography. There is a danger of exaggerating the extent to which both Panaetius and Posidonius really disagreed with the fundamental tenets of the school. Nor should we underestimate the extent to which a writer like Cicero – not himself a Stoic, but greatly influenced by Stoic ideas – could himself give Greek thought a new, Roman slant. Subsequently, under the Empire, the leading Stoic writers (Seneca, c. 4 BC/AD 1–AD 65, the tutor of the Emperor Nero; Epictetus, c. AD 55–135; Marcus Aurelius, AD 121–180 and himself Emperor from AD 161) laid particular emphasis on the ethical teachings of the school.

Scepticism

A greater or less degree of scepticism about the possibility of achieving certain knowledge of the world had been present in many Greek thinkers even before the Hellenistic period. Scepticism as a distinctive philosophical tradition, leading to tranquillity and happiness through suspension of judgement, was however connected by later writers above all with Pyrrho of Elis (c.365/360–275/270 BC). Pyrrho himself, like Socrates, wrote nothing; his teachings were recorded by his follower Timon of Phlius, and these works themselves survive only in secondary quotations.

Scepticism was taken up by Plato's school, the Academy, first under Arcesilaus (316–242 BC) and then under Carneades (214–129 BC), who went on an embassy from Athens to Rome in 155 BC and there scandalised the elder Cato by arguing for and then against justice on successive days. (Cicero adapted these arguments in the third book of his *Republic*, but reversed the order.) A reading of Plato's early Socratic dialogues as leading to scepticism is perhaps not an unnatural one. The Academic sceptics attacked Stoic arguments and claimed that on the Stoics' own principles suspension of judgement was the only reasonable course. Our evidence is again secondary, much of it from Cicero, who was an adherent of the school. Cicero's philosophical dialogues expound both Epicurean and Stoic positions and then reject them as uncertain, though his inclination is towards Stoicism rather than Epicureanism. He refers to the (sceptical) Academic practice of arguing both for and against a position as a good training for the orator (Cicero, *Tusculan Disputations* 2.9); it was perhaps particularly congenial to him as a lawyer.

Already by Cicero's time, however, Academic scepticism was

becoming more moderate, as we will see in Chapter Two. Pyrrhonian scepticism was revived by Aenesidemus (first century BC) and given its fullest expression, as far as texts known to us are concerned, in the writings of Sextus Empiricus (c.AD 200). Under the Roman Empire dogmatic Platonism revived in the Greek East, and there was renewed interest in the teachings and writings of Aristotle; but both these developments fall outside the main concerns of the present book. The period of the later Republic and the early Empire has often been described as one of philosophical eclecticism; we should rather think of different traditions engaging in debate and influencing one another, with Stoicism perhaps the most widely known, until the rise of Neoplatonism in the third century AD.

As will have become clear from this account, the history of the various schools is complex and the nature of the sources creates problems of its own. But these points can perhaps best be illustrated by turning to the discussion of specific doctrines.

2

HOW DO WE KNOW ANYTHING?

EMPIRICISM

In the fifth century BC Parmenides had argued that knowledge is to be achieved through reasoning rather than through the senses. In the fourth century Plato had claimed, in his *Phaedo*, that the most the senses can do is to remind us of realities accessible only to reason – Platonic 'Forms' - the memories of which are already present in our souls when they enter human bodies, though not conscious until we recollect them. Plato based this claim on our ability to work out *a priori* mathematical truths without prior experience of them and on our ability to know and prove (rather than just suppose) whether or not we have the correct answer. He extended the model to other kinds of knowledge too, such as ethics, where its application is more questionable. If one accepts Plato's view, it follows that suppositions we make on the basis of sense-experience can therefore be at best just that, suppositions; certainty must come from elsewhere, from apprehension of the Forms by our reason and by recollection of that apprehension – though it is only fair to say that in later dialogues, notably the *Theaetetus*, Plato continued to concern himself with just what distinguishes knowledge known to be true from opinion that happens to be so, and does not simply claim that appeal to the Forms and to antenatal intuition are enough on their own to provide a solution to the problem.

Aristotle rejected Platonic recollection along with the pre-existence of the soul, and argued that knowledge of first principles (from which other truths can then be demonstrated by argument) is built up from repeated sense-experiences. But he shows relatively little concern for the problem of how we can be sure that we have

11

achieved knowledge; presumably this is because he supposes that, in a universe where, in his view, organisation directed towards the achieving of goals is the norm, human nature itself is such that we have the capacity for understanding things correctly.[1] Consistently with this, he holds that any view that has been held either by many people or by acknowledged experts is likely to have some truth in it; the way to achieve understanding is to consider established views on a question and to develop an explanation that accounts for them even if not accepting them in their entirety.[2]

Both the Epicureans and the Stoics share the view that knowledge is ultimately based on sense-experience; the mind at birth is a blank (Aristotle had himself used the image of a blank writing-tablet, *On the Soul* 3.4 430a1) and it is only from sense-experience that concepts and opinions, whether accurate or not, can enter into it. But they were more exercised than Aristotle apparently was by the question how we can be sure of anything; and while both schools used arguments from the common agreement of (almost) all human beings, for example to show that gods exist, in practice they very soon parted company from common opinion, and from each other, on further questions such as the nature of those gods.

EPICURUS

For Epicurus, as for the earlier atomist Democritus, vision involves films of atoms ('images', *eidôla*) constantly being thrown off from the surface of every object and travelling through the air towards our eyes. (For Epicurus the images simply impinge upon our eyes; Democritus' position was more complex, arguing that the stream of atoms from the object met with another stream sent out by our eyes and combined to produce an image in mid-air between us and the object. It was a not uncommon belief in ancient Greece that rays of light issued *from* people's eyes. Cf. KRS 589.) The image affects the 'soul'-atoms in our eyes and is transmitted from there to the mind; the whole process is to be understood in material terms, of patterns of atoms and their movements and rearrangements. (More on this, and the problems it raises, in Chapters Three and Four; it may be helpful to modern readers to think of the process in terms of patterns of electrical impulses in the nerves, so long as we are aware that the mechanism postulated by Epicurus was different, though equally physical.)

For Epicurus, all sensations, as such, are true (Lucretius, 4.499 = LS 16A; DL 10.31–2 = LS 16B). This initially surprising claim can be better understood if we relate it to the physical mechanism by which sensation occurs. Consider two favourite examples in ancient discussion, the straight oar partly in and partly out of the water which looks bent, or the square tower which looks round at a distance because of haze (even in the clarity of the ancient Greek air). For Epicurus, what has happened is that the image has been distorted in each case while travelling from the object to our eyes; that of the tower has quite literally had its corners knocked off by collision with the atoms of the intervening air (Lucretius, 4.353ff. = LS 16G). Therefore what we actually experience, what impinges on us, is indeed in the one case the image of a bent oar, in the other that of a round tower (not in the sense that the image actually *comes from* a round tower, but in the sense that it is an image that would have had to come from a round tower if it had represented its source accurately). (But, while the image is what impinges on us, what we *see* is not the image but the tower – imperfectly, in this case – by means of the image.)[3] Indeed the visions even of madmen are real, in the sense that images corresponding to what they suppose they see really do impinge upon them, though not in fact originating from the things from which they appear to originate. The reality of the experience is shown by the effects it produces in those who undergo it, for – a general Epicurean tenet – only what is real and physical can produce a movement (DL 10.32 = LS 16B). Error arises not in the sensation itself but in 'the addition of opinion' – that is, in our assuming too soon that the actual object, the oar or the tower, really is the same shape as the image that reaches us (*ad Hdt.* 50–1 = LS 15A).

In the case of visible objects confirmation or 'attestation' can be achieved by getting a 'clear vision' (*enargeia*) of the object – in the case of the tower, pretty clearly, by waiting until we can get a closer look at it. But there are three sorts of case where it is not possible to do this through the senses. One is that of the heavenly bodies and meteorological phenomena such as thunder and lightning, which are too remote for us to get a clear vision of them; the second is that of the minute atomic particles from which everything, ourselves included, is made up, and which are too small to be directly apprehended themselves by the senses; the third is that of the gods.

In the case of heavenly phenomena, Epicurus argues that we

13

should accept *every* explanation compatible with the evidence of our senses; to do otherwise, when we have no grounds on which to choose between them, would, he says, be to engage in 'myth' (*Letter to Pythocles* 87 = LS 18C). Moreover, Epicurus believes, as had Democritus, that both time and space are infinite (see Chapter Three) and that an infinite number of world-systems (of which our 'solar' system is one, except that Epicurus, like most ancient Greeks, placed the earth rather than the sun at the centre) come into being, last for a time, and then perish. Thus, it seems, *any* possible explanation will be true in some world system even if not in ours. (Cf. Lucretius, 5.526ff. = LS 18D.) Indeed, by the principle of *isonomia* or 'equilibrium', what is rare in one part of the universe must be frequent elsewhere (Lucretius, 2.532ff.; Cicero, *On the Nature of the Gods* 1.50, cf. LS vol. 2 pp. 148–9).

Epicurus' reluctance here to go beyond the limitations of our evidence may seem commendably 'scientific'. However, qualifications are needed. First, Epicurus' particular interest in heavenly phenomena explicitly arises from his desire to argue that they are not signs of divine wisdom or anger, and that the gods have no concern with our world at all: 'First of all we must not think that there is any other aim in knowledge of heavenly phenomena, whether in combination [with other subjects] or in isolation, than peace of mind and firm assurance' (*Letter to Pythocles* 85–7 = LS 18C). Thunder and lightning had long been associated with the gods; more recently Plato and his followers had argued (see [Plato], *Epinomis* 983e ff.) that worship of the heavenly bodies, shown to be divine and good by the regularity of their movements, was the appropriate form of religion for ordinary people who could not rise, as philosophers could, above the level of adoring physical things. And what the explanations of heavenly phenomena that Epicurus admits as possible have in common is that they exclude any form of divine involvement. The basis for this must be that such divine involvement is incompatible with the argument that concern for the world is incompatible with the gods' tranquil happiness (see Chapter Three). Moreover, Epicurus (as represented in the *Letter to Pythocles*), and following him Lucretius, admit not only astronomical theories which were recent when Epicurus wrote, but also crude theories from the sixth century BC which no one any longer took seriously. When we read that the sun may be rekindled anew every day, and that if you go to the top of Mount Ida in Turkey and look out to the east you can see this happening

(Lucretius, 5.663; though to be fair he does say 'there is a story ... '), we may conclude that the criteria for possible explanations are theological rather than scientific; and the impression that Epicureanism is interested in inquiries concerning nature as a means to an end rather than as an end in themselves is reinforced by the indications that some of Epicurus' lists of alternative explanations were taken from followers of Aristotle whose interest in such explanation *was* scientific, concerned with the more accurate classifying of phenomena.[4]

Where atoms and void themselves are concerned, there can for Epicurus be no possibility of direct sensation at all; the colours that we see, for example, are produced by the arrangement of atoms in the films that impinge on us, and an individual atom cannot have an arrangement in this sense. Indeed it is not even the case that a particular *shape* of an individual atom goes with a particular colour (Lucretius, 2.817). The only properties that individual atoms have are shape, weight and size and the necessary concomitants of shape (*ad Hdt.* 54 = LS 12D); the only things they can do are to move through void and collide with other atoms. Sight and the other senses can only exist on the level of the complex interactions of compounds made up of many atoms in particular arrangements.

Therefore, whereas in the case of clearly visible objects we should accept those impressions that are attested by the evidence of the senses in a clear vision, and reject those that are not attested, in the case of things that cannot be clearly observed we should accept those that are *not contested* by the evidence of the senses, and reject those that are contested. What this means can best be illustrated by two examples, those of the existence of void and of the swerving of atoms from their paths. Motion, Epicurus argued as had Democritus, is only possible if there is empty space. (Lucretius, 1.370ff. = LS 6A. Others had argued that motion was possible by mutual replacement, as if the water displaced by the head of a fish swimming forwards at once moves round in sequence, filling up the space left by its tail; but this the atomists rejected.) It therefore follows that empty space must exist, even though we cannot sense it directly; for its non-existence is contested by the evidence of the senses.[5] For the senses show that motion occurs; and reason shows (it is claimed) that motion is impossible without void. Void and body are mutually exclusive, so that if void exists there must also be bodies small enough to contain no void at all; these will be physically indivisible, *because* they contain no void (cf. *ad Hdt*. 41; Lucretius, 1.532ff. = LS 8B). That is to say, they will be atoms (the Greek word *atomos* simply meaning 'indivisible' or more literally 'uncuttable'). And thus, whereas for heavenly phenomena there are alternative possible explanations, for the structure of matter that underlies our sense-experience there is one and only one, the atomic theory. (This is not indeed the only Epicurean argument for the existence of atoms; others will be considered in Chapter Three.)

The claim that motion is impossible without empty space presumably itself rests on analogy with our sense-experience: we can only rearrange objects within a box if there is some 'empty' space within the box to enable us to start. The space will not of course be empty of all atoms; it is what we call 'empty' on the level of our experience, but may serve as an analogy. Indeed analogy is central to Epicurean argument about atoms and void, which we cannot experience directly; in using images from sense-experience, which he does repeatedly, Lucretius is not just giving a poetic vividness to his exposition, but following the principles of Epicurean epistemology. But analogies can mislead. The objects in the box are a good analogy for the discrete units – atoms – out of which Epicurus supposes all things are constituted. If, however, matter were physically infinitely divisible, it might seem that the requirement of void for there to be movement would be less obvious[6] – though against this it might in turn be objected that the burden of argument is on those who make such a claim to indicate what motion *would* be like on their view.

The second, more surprising, example of non-contestation is that of the swerving of atoms from their paths. There are two reasons why Epicurus argues this must occur: first, if all atoms initially fell straight downwards in parallel lines, some swerve at least would be needed for collisions and reboundings to begin and compounds to be created; second, the swerve is needed to explain human free will. These arguments will be examined in more detail later, in Chapters Three and Four respectively; for the present the relevant point to note is that, according to Lucretius (2.249 = LS 11H), the swerve is something that is not contested by sense-experience. The senses show that falling bodies, left to their own devices, fall in approximately straight lines; but they cannot show that no deviation at all occurs, though it must be very slight. Once again, reason – itself ultimately based on sensory experience of the

16

existence of compounds and of free will – has certain requirements; the direct evidence of the senses does not contest the theory that reason requires.

At this point a comparison with the earlier atomist Democritus may be instructive. While Epicurus held that all sensations were true, Democritus had held that they could not give us genuine knowledge at all, and that for two reasons. First because, unlike Epicurus, he held that only atoms and void were real; the properties of compounds, for Democritus, existed only as *conventional* descriptions of the effects they have on us (KRS 549, cf. 554). And second, our perception of things through the senses is affected not only by the atomic constitution of the object we perceive, but also by our own atomic make-up; different people will experience the same thing in different ways according as their own constitution differs (KRS 553).

On the face of it, then, Epicurus' theory of knowledge is diametrically opposed to Democritus'. But in practice they seem to have been very similar. Democritus, no less than Epicurus, held that all knowledge must ultimately be based on the senses, and that if the senses are rejected there will be no other foundation for knowledge to build upon (Democritus, KRS 552; Epicurus, *PD* 23 = LS 16D; Lucretius, 4.469 = LS 16A).

The difference is really one of emphasis and context. Democritus was reacting to Parmenides and his follower Melissus, who had argued that reason showed that movement was impossible and that the senses, which give us the impression that things move, were therefore unreliable; in particular, Melissus had argued that empty space, as not-being, could not exist, and that motion was impossible for this reason. Democritus, like Epicurus after him, is arguing that the conclusions of reason have to be judged by the evidence of the senses; since movement clearly does occur, reason must produce a theory – that of atoms and the void – which can account for it. The difference is that Democritus, being closer to Parmenides than Epicurus is, emphasises the role of reasoning in his theory, while arguing against Parmenides that reason must take account of the evidence of the senses. Democritus, unlike Parmenides, can account for the objects of sense-experience, such as colour, but he nevertheless regards them as secondary. For Epicurus, on the other hand, atomic compounds – the objects of our experience – and their colours are just as *real* as the underlying atoms separated by void that go to make them up. They are real, but on a different level. This point will be important later (see Chapter Four).

So far, in Epicurus' theory, we have been dealing with objects experienced through the senses and with the conclusions of reasoning about atoms and void which we cannot apprehend directly at all. The position, is however, complicated by Epicurus' recognition of images of finer atomic structure which do not affect our senses but act directly upon our minds, passing straight through our bodily structure to our minds (which are as physical as every other part of us, made up of atoms and located, according to a common though not universal ancient Greek belief, in our chests. If it were not for this location it might be more helpful for the modern reader to think of the brain, a physical organ, rather than the mind). These images acting directly upon our minds are invoked first to explain our awareness of the gods, but also to explain images 'seen' in dreams – visions of people who have died and no longer exist (thus showing that visions in dreams of people who have died are not evidence for the soul's survival somewhere after death), and also dream images of impossible creatures such as centaurs, which result from images that are real enough but have coalesced in ways that do not reflect the original objects from which they come.[7]

However, this theory of finer atomic images apprehensible only to the mind and not to the senses also had a further, bizarre application. For Epicurus, as for Aristotle, concepts – called by Epicurus 'presuppositions' or *prolêpseis* – are stored up in our minds as a result of experience, stored presumably as atomic configurations (a fragment of Diogenes of Oenoanda's inscription speaks of 'passages' opened in us by sense-experience: fr. 9.III Smith = LS 15E). And according to one text, admittedly a report by Diogenes Laertius (10.32 = LS 15F) and not in Epicurus' own words, further concepts can be built up from these by such processes as analogy and combination. The picture then might seem simple: I have in my mind a conception of a horse, say, built up from seeing many horses, and if I want to think of a horse when none is actually visible to me I simply activate the stored concept. And from this one might suppose that the notion of a centaur simply results from the combination of concepts of human and horse in our minds. However, we have already seen that this is not in fact how Epicurus explains our thinking of centaurs; and his account of what happens when I think of a horse is not what one might expect it to be either. For he apparently claims that I can think of a horse whenever I want to because there are innumerable fine images of everything, accessible to our minds but not to our senses, flying about everywhere all the time, so that whenever I want to think of a horse my mind can easily grab the image of one from the constant stream of images of all sorts (Lucretius, 4.779ff. = LS 15D). Thought-images of horses can presumably pass through solid walls, whereas visual images cannot; there are some, indeed very many, of the former in the room where you are reading this now, but probably none of the latter, unless a horse is just passing the window.

However, the stored preconception will presumably still be needed to ensure that I grab the right image, one that is indeed of a horse; indeed, it would seem to be needed for me to form the desire to think of a horse in the first place. Presumably the right image will be grabbed because it will fit into the passages opened up by previous experience; since these passages are produced by previous sensation, empiricism is not compromised. Nevertheless, the involvement of external thought-images seems to introduce a certain amount of redundancy into the theory. Epicurus seems here to be taking to extremes the idea that not only sensations but even thoughts must have a direct basis in objective reality, even if they do not always reflect accurately the objects from which they came.

According to Diogenes Laertius (10.31–2 = LS 17A), Epicurus recognised three criteria of truth, sensation, feelings (i.e. pleasure and pain) and preconceptions (*prolêpseis*); his followers added 'impression-applications of the intellect' (*phantastikai epibolai tês dianoias*). The situation may in fact be simpler than this suggests. Of the three criteria attributed to Epicurus himself, feelings are in effect sensations of the state of one's own body and mind, and preconceptions are, as we have seen, ultimately founded upon sensations. As for the 'impression-applications of the intellect', these were doubtless introduced to cater for cases like those of the gods, apprehended by images directly affecting the mind, rather than through the senses. Attempts have been made to interpret the expression in such a way as to give Epicurus a criterion of truth depending upon mental intuition and thus to overthrow his general sense-based empiricism, but these are not convincing.

THE STOICS

The fundamentals of the Stoic theory of knowledge are remarkably similar to those of the Epicurean theory. Stoic views on physics, as we shall see in Chapter Three, are in many respects diametrically opposed to those of Epicurus – for example, for the Stoics there is no void within the cosmos, and matter is a continuum rather than being made up of discrete particles – and so it is hardly surprising that the *mechanism* of sensation is very different; vision, for example, is explained not by the travelling of images from the seen object to our eye, but by the 'tensioning' of a cone of 'spirit' (*pneuma*) whose vertex is at the eye and whose base is the seen object (DL 7.157 = LS 53N; more on *pneuma* in Chapter Three). But, different though the mechanism may be, the subsequent story is similar: the mind is a blank at birth ('Aëtius' 4.11.1 = LS 39E),[8] and repeated sensations give rise to concepts stored within the mind. The account of the ways in which more complex concepts can develop is very similar to that attributed to Epicurus:

> Of conceptions some are from encounter, some from similarity, some from analogy, some from transposition, some from combination, some from opposition. Conceptions of perceptible things are from encounter; from similarity those which derive from something that is present, as Socrates from his statue; from analogy, some by increase, like Tityus and the Cyclops, some by diminution, like a pigmy. And the centre of the earth is conceived of by analogy from smaller spheres. From transposition, for example eyes on the breast [sc. in fabulous monsters]; from combination the conception of the Hippocentaur originated;[9] and from opposition, that of death. Some conceptions are also from a certain transference, like *lekta* and place. And the conception of something just and good arises naturally. And by privation, like what is without hands.

> (DL 7.53 = LS 39D)

Indeed, the Stoics even borrowed Epicurus' very word 'preconceptions' (*prolêpseis*). However, they applied it particularly to concepts that arise naturally,[10] placing more emphasis than did Epicurus on the distinction between these and those that are developed from them (the general word for all concepts being *ennoiai*). They also laid emphasis on a class of 'common notions', *koinai ennoiai*, shared by all human beings, using the common opinion of mankind, for instance, as an argument not only for the existence of the gods (Cicero, *On the Nature of the Gods* 2.12 = LS 54C) but also for their providential care (Plutarch, *CN* 1075E = LS 54K).

When the text quoted above says that a conception of what is just and good is 'natural' (*phusikôs noeitai dikaion ti kai agathon*), this should not be understood in terms of an innate idea of goodness, which would conflict with the principle that the mind at birth is a blank. What is meant is rather that this conception *develops* naturally. How it does so we will see in Chapter Five; Seneca, who in *Letters on Morals* 120.3ff. = LS 60E describes the process, states explicitly that nature gives us seeds of knowledge rather than knowledge itself. It may thus be appropriate, in this case and in that of other concepts too, to speak of innate capacities or tendencies in human beings, but the important point is that the validation of our knowledge is not otherworldly, as it is in full-blown Platonism.[11] That the way in which we experience and learn from the world depends in part on our own nature is hardly surprising in the context of the Stoic system, in which our individual natures are in any case part of a larger whole (as we shall see in Chapter Three). It may raise the question how we can be sure that our natures do not prevent us from apprehending the truth; but the Stoic answer will presumably be an enhanced version of that already suggested for Aristotle. In a universe which, in the Stoic view, not only manifests purposeful arrangement but is providentially ordered in every detail, it is natural to suppose that human beings – the highest form of life in it apart from the gods – are constructed in such a way that they are capable of apprehending what is true. The problem is rather why so many people, according to the Stoics, fail to such a great extent to do so; but that is a problem to which we shall have to return repeatedly in its various guises.

There are three important areas in which Stoic 'logic' went beyond Epicurean 'canonic'. The first concerns the basis of certainty. For Epicurus, it will be remembered, error arises from jumping to conclusions about what we sense, rather than waiting for the 'clear vision'. No rules were laid down for determining when a vision is or is not clear; this is presumably meant to be itself a matter of experience and common sense. The Stoics, however, went further, arguing that certain impressions or 'presentations'

21

(*phantasiai*) are such that they *could not* mislead us; 'apprehensive' or 'cognitive' impressions, *katalêptikai phantasiai*, are such that they could not have come from anything other than that from which they in fact come (Sextus, *M* 7.248 = LS 40E.3).

When an impression impinges upon us, we have a choice whether to assent to it or not. (Strictly speaking, we assent not to the impression of fruit in the bowl that is good to eat, but to a proposition corresponding to it, that there is fruit in the bowl that is good to eat. But nothing significant depends on this point for the present argument.) A foolish person will assent to non-apprehensive impressions; a wise person, or 'sage', only to apprehensive ones, suspending judgement otherwise. Assent to an apprehensive impression constitutes apprehension or cognition; the unwise person's ill-founded or 'weak' assent to a non-apprehensive impression is mere opinion.[12] (More on the Stoic sage and the ordinary, unwise person in Chapter Five.) Zeno, the founder of the Stoic school, illustrated sensation by the outstretched hand, assent by the curled fingers, apprehension by the closed fist and knowledge by the grasping of one hand by the other (Cicero, *Academica Priora* 2.145 = LS 41A); for knowledge for the Stoics is part of a whole system, and while individual statements can be true (or false), *truth*, as opposed to just 'what is true', is a property of the system as a whole.

The problem is, of course, that while we receive many impressions of which we can be reasonably sure that they represent their sources accurately, it is less easy to find examples of individual impressions which simply *could not* be in any way distorted or misleading – especially when sceptical critics are trying to catch you out with bowls of wax fruit and the like, of which more later. In effect, by making so definite their claim that certain identifiable impressions could not mislead, the Stoics were making themselves more open to sceptical attack than they would otherwise have been. Later Stoics indeed, under pressure from the Academic sceptics, modified the definition so as to include the provision that an apprehensive presentation was one that had no obstacle to its being apprehended. A man can normally recognise his own wife without there being any doubt about the matter; but this was not so for Admetus in Euripides' play when his wife Alcestis had returned from the dead (Sextus, *M* 7.253 = LS 40K. Admetus was not indeed a Stoic sage; but that is irrelevant to the question whether the impression was apprehensive or not).

The example may prompt the question, how can we ever be sure whether or not there is an obstacle in any given case? But the effect of an obstacle need only be to cause withholding assent – in Admetus' case, to the impression 'this is my wife' – not to cause rash assent. We need not suppose that the sage in these circumstances will rashly assent to an alternative proposition, e.g. 'since this cannot be my wife, it must be a phantom sent by the gods'; he may simply withhold judgement, which is what he should always do when there is no apprehensive presentation. The fact that the sage in circumstances like Admetus' might not realise that the person who looks like his wife is in fact his wife after all, and so suspends judgement, is not an argument for universal suspension of judgement. What is needed for this is the thought that on *every* occasion there *might* be considerations which should lead one to withhold judgement, even though there is nothing on the face of it to suggest that in fact there are; and that goes beyond the Admetus example, where the obstacle to assent is itself apparent.

The second important Stoic contribution to 'logic', in their own broad sense of the term, was their theory of the *lekton* or 'that which is said'. Consider Cato walking, and someone who says out loud in Latin, with Cato in view but without pointing to him, 'Cato ambulat' ('Cato is walking'). A person who does not know Latin will see the walking Cato – who is a physical object – and will hear the sounds the speaker utters, which are also physical objects (modifications of the air). But he or she will not connect the sounds with the physical object Cato behaving in a certain way, and has thus failed to apprehend a third, incorporeal thing, the *lekton* or what the words are actually *saying* (Seneca, *Letters on Morals* 117.13 = LS 33E).

The recognition that there is a third, intermediary thing connecting speech (or thought, regarded as silent speech, but still a physical modification of the mind) and the physical objects to which it refers was a major advance (the point not being understood by Aristotle, for example, for whom words simply reflect thoughts and thoughts correspond, or fail to correspond, to external objects). It seems indeed to anticipate the modern distinction between sense and reference. This has been questioned, on the grounds that there were no *lekta* corresponding to nouns, only to complete propositions (as in our example) and to predicates such as 'is walking', the latter being 'incomplete *lekta*'. However, there is one passage, Sextus, *M* 8.11–12 = LS 33B, which makes a similar point to the one from Seneca cited above, but does so with the example not of a complete sentence but of the noun, in fact a proper name, 'Dion'; and Michael Frede has argued that 'case', interpreted by LS p. 201 as indicating for the Stoics a noun in one or another grammatical case, i.e., a *word*, was understood as standing for a quality (on which cf. Chapter Three) even in counterfactual circumstances where the quality was not actually present. It is thus not strictly a *lekton*, for to name Dion is not to make a *statement*, but it can form part of a complete *lekton*.[13]

Third, whereas Epicurus rejected the formal study of logic, the Stoics developed a system of logic that was more fundamental than Aristotle's, though this was not realised until similar principles had been developed independently in the nineteenth century. The Stoics were building on the work of Aristotle's followers Theophrastus and Eudemus, but saw its significance in a way that Theophrastus and Eudemus themselves did not. Whereas Aristotelian logic is concerned with the interrelations of terms ('all human beings are mortal, all Greeks are human beings, so all Greeks are mortal') Stoic logic is concerned with the interrelations of propositions ('if it is day, it is light: but it is day: so it is light', and 'if it is day, it is light: but it is not light: so it is not day'). Argument-forms like those of which these are examples (they are in fact the first two of Chrysippus' five fundamental or 'undemonstrated' argument-forms, for which cf. Sextus, *PH* 2.156–9, *M* 8.224ff.; DL 7.79 = LS 36A) were indeed *used* by Aristotle to demonstrate points in his logic, but were not made part of his formal system. In the Middle Ages these two argument-forms became known respectively as *modus ponendo ponens* and *modus tollendo tollens*. (The superficially similar form, 'if the first then the second: but not the first: so not the second' – the Stoics used numbers as propositional variables – is not valid unless one has 'if *and only if* the first, then the second'; otherwise its use constitutes the fallacy of 'affirming the consequent', as in 'if it is morning, it is light: but it is not morning: so it is not light', or the equivalent 'if it is morning, it is light: but it is light: so it is morning'. Or, since the fallacy is and always has been much loved by politicians, consider the formally equivalent 'if you are idle and/or incompetent, you will not approve of performance-related pay: but you do not approve of performance-related pay: so you are idle and/or incompetent'. The fact that all the statements in each case may as it happens be true, or not, is beside the point; what is important for *logical* argument is whether or not the argument-form is valid.) The Stoics, and above all Chrysippus, developed these principles into a whole system of logic, with rules for the reduction of complex arguments to their simpler constituents, anticipating the modern propositional calculus.

One issue of importance was the conditions for the truth of a conditional statement (cf. Sextus, *M* 2.110ff. = LS 35B); here the Stoics were developing the insights of the Dialectical philosophers. Philo (early third century BC) argued that a conditional statement was true provided that the antecedent was not true and the consequent false; this is equivalent to the 'material implication' of modern logic.[14] Philonian conditionals share with material implication the paradoxes that a true statement can be implied by anything and that a false statement can imply anything. (For, in daytime, neither 'if 2 + 2 = 5, it is daytime' nor 'if 2 + 2 = 5, it is night' has a true antecedent and a false consequent, and having that combination is the only way in which, on this definition, a conditional can be falsified.) Philo's teacher, Diodorus Cronus (died c.284 BC) held rather that a true conditional is one which neither has nor will ever have a true antecedent and a false consequent; but this still leaves conditionals as truth-functional and subject to the paradoxes of material implication (consider 'if 2 + 2 = 5, the Pope is male'; or, Sextus' actual example, 'if there are no atoms, there are atoms', which never has a false consequent – at least if you are an atomist).

Sextus Empiricus records two further definitions of truth in conditionals, of which the first is probably the standard Stoic view. It is that a conditional is true if the negation of its consequent is incompatible with its antecedent (which does not apply to 'if 2 + 2 = 5, the Pope is male'; however exactly 'incompatible' is to be defined, the Pope's being female is hardly *incompatible* with 2 + 2 equalling 5). The significance for Chrysippus of the contrast between the negated disjunction, 'not both … ', and the conditional with 'if' will concern us again in Chapter Three. The second, perhaps over-restrictive definition is that a conditional is true if and only if the consequent is 'contained in' the antecedent; we are not given positive examples of what this amounts to, only told that it would exclude repetitive conditionals like 'if it is day it is day' (for identity is not containment).

Such repetitive forms of argument had much to do with the decline of Stoic logic in later antiquity. Aristotle and his later followers saw logic as a practical instrument (*organon*), and Stoic argument-forms of this type were dismissed as pointless (cf. e.g. Alexander of Aphrodisias, *On Aristotle's* Prior Analytics 284.10ff.:

> It is also possible to take three syllogisms from the three [Aristotelian] figures which are overlapping and overlapped according to the theorem of composition which has been handed down. Aristotle and his followers, taking usefulness as their measure, handed it down only to the extent that this required, but the Stoics took it over from them and, dividing it up, made from it what they call the second, third and fourth *themata*, disregarding usefulness, but investigating and being jealous concerning everything that can in whatever way be said in such a study, even if it is useless.

As an example of an apparently useless argument one may cite the syllogism that is 'valid without a difference', such as 'either the first or the second: but the first: so the first', where the conclusion indicates nothing more than the second premiss (cf. LS p. 220). But the Stoics were interested in such arguments for the sake of logical form in itself, and discovered arguments not without interest such as the following (Origen, *Against Celsus* 7.15 = LS 36F):

> If you know you are dead, you are dead.
> If you know you are dead, you are not dead
> Therefore not: you know that you are dead

(assuming the premisses 'anything someone knows must be true' and 'only living people can know anything'); or, conversely, (Sextus, *M* 8.281, cf. 8.466, *PH* 2.186)

> If a sign exists, a sign exists.
> If a sign does not exist, a sign exists.
> But a sign either does not exist or exists.
> Therefore a sign exists

(for if no sign exists, there must be some sign that no sign exists). The second of these is an anticipation of the medieval *consequentia mirabilis*.[15]

Aristotelian logic nevertheless prevailed, largely because it was taken up by the Neoplatonists, and propositional logic had to be rediscovered. Given the minimal nature of punctuation in early manuscripts, sentences like 'if if it is day it is light and it is day it is light' (the conditionalised form of 'if it is day it is light: but it is day: so it is light') had been natural candidates for textual corruption.[16]

It would be a mistake, however, to see the Stoics as interested in logic purely as a formal system. It is the study of the operations of reason; the divine reason that governs the world and of which our souls are parts, as we shall see in Chapters Three and Four, follows the same rules. Indeed correlations can be seen between the formulations of Stoic logic, on the one hand, and the structure of the world as a nexus of causes and effects and the way in which we experience it, on the other. More on this in Chapter Three.

THE SCEPTICS

As explained in Chapter One, Academic scepticism is a turning of the Stoics' principles against themselves. The Stoics themselves recognise that, when an impression is not certain or 'apprehensive', the sage will suspend judgement; if there are in fact no apprehensive impressions, the wise thing to do is to suspend judgement all the time. Arcesilaus turned this argument against the Stoics and argued that by the Stoics' own principles the sage will *always* suspend judgement (Sextus, *M* 7.155 = LS 41C). The point is illustrated by the story of the discomfiture of a Stoic philosopher. Ptolemy Philopator, the king of Egypt, had a bowl of wax pomegranates served to the Stoic Sphaerus; when Sphaerus took a piece of fruit to taste, Ptolemy cried out that he had assented to a false impression. Sphaerus replied that he had assented not to the proposition that they were pomegranates, but only to the proposition that it was reasonable for them to be pomegranates (DL 7.177 = LS 40F). One of the puzzles about the story is why Sphaerus should have been ashamed to admit he had made a false judgement, for only the Stoic sage was supposed to be infallible, and the sage was as rare as the phoenix – no Stoic ever claimed to be a sage himself, though Socrates was regarded as having been such, and some leading Stoics were regarded as sages by later generations of the school. But, this point aside (which I owe to Tad Brennan), Sphaerus' response simply strengthens the sceptic case, for it suggests that it is never wise to give assent to any unqualified proposition. The question is whether we should accept the implication. Long and Sedley argue (p. 252) that the Academic argument does not go far enough, for it needs to show not just

27

that there are some circumstances in which apparently reliable appearances may be misleading, but that every case is potentially like this. The Academic sceptic will reply that the recognition that there are some cases where apparently reliable evidence is not in fact so is enough to ensure that, even if we may sometimes, or even often, as a matter of fact be correct in the conclusions we draw from the evidence of our senses, we cannot be sure *when* this is so. (It is also true that for the Stoics there is *some* difference between any two non-identical things. This should imply that we will never mistake one thing for another if we examine it closely enough.[17] However, a critic might not accept the premiss, and in any case the implication that the sage should suspend judgement until all possible differences have been checked seems to make the difference between the Stoic position and the Academic one retreat to vanishing point.)

Arcesilaus, holding that truth was unattainable, made 'what is reasonable' the criterion that should govern our conduct (Sextus, *M* 7.158 = LS 69B). Carneades spoke rather of what is 'persuasive' or 'plausible' (Greek *pithanos*); this was rendered into Latin by Cicero as *probabilis*, but the associations of English 'probable' may be misleading, for it is a matter of subjective acceptability rather than, for example, of probability as objective likelihood expressed in quantitative terms. In more important matters Carneades' full description of the criterion was the impression which was 'persuasive, and uncontroverted, and thoroughly examined' (Sextus, *M* 7.166, 184 = LS 69D, E).

Philo of Larisa, who succeeded Carneades' pupil Clitomachus as head of the Academy in 110/109 BC, argued that things were 'not apprehensible by the Stoic criterion, but were apprehensible as far as the nature of things themselves is concerned' (Sextus, *PH* 1.235 = LS 68T), and further claimed that this had been the consistent position of the Academy throughout (Cicero, *Academica* 1.13 = LS 68B). This conflation of the early, dogmatic Academy of Plato and his immediate successors with the later, sceptical Academy angered Philo's pupil Antiochus of Ascalon, who rejected scepticism altogether and adopted the Stoic epistemology. (Cf. Cicero, *Academica* 2.132: 'Antiochus ... was called an Academic but was, if he had changed a very few things, a most genuine Stoic'; Sextus, *PH* 1.235 = LS 68T. More on Antiochus in Chapter Five.)

Antiochus has often been seen as restoring dogmatic Platonism, and Philo – not least by the supporters of Antiochus in antiquity, as in Cicero, *Academica* 2.18 = LS 68U – as advocating only a feeble and failed compromise. But, as Tarrant has pointed out, it may have been Philo who was the more authentic Platonist and who laid the foundations for the revival of dogmatic Platonism. To say with Antiochus that things can be apprehended for certain by the Stoic criterion – that is, by sense-impressions, and particularly by the alleged 'apprehensive' ones – is hardly Platonic; and Philo's claim that things can be apprehended 'in themselves' sounds like a claim that we can know the general natures of things even if we cannot be certain of individual instances, and that is at least a part of the point of the Platonic Theory of Forms.[18] Plato, indeed, refers to Forms such as Beauty and Justice as 'the beautiful *itself*' and 'the just *itself*'.

'Pyrrhonian' scepticism, which we know best through the writings of Sextus, took an even more extreme position, suspending judgement altogether concerning the external world. It should be stressed at the outset that – as Sextus himself is at pains to point out – the Sceptic (the term will be used for the rest of this chapter specifically to refer to the Pyrrhonian or neo-Pyrrhonian sceptic as represented in Sextus) is prepared to make assertions about his own sense-experiences; his scepticism concerns only assertions about the external world (Sextus, *PH* 1.19–20; DL 9.104–5 = LS 1H). Nor does the ancient Sceptic as represented by Sextus, at least, share Cartesian doubts about existence; it is not, it would seem, the existence even of an external reality that is doubted (let alone of oneself) but the possibility of knowing anything for certain about its nature.[19] On the other hand, Sextus' scepticism is not just scepticism about claims to knowledge; suspension of judgement excludes even the holding of opinions and the making of any statements expressing commitment about anything beyond one's own experiences. It does not follow that if we did make such statements we would not sometimes be right; but since there have never yet in our experience been conclusive reasons for making any assertion rather than its opposite,[20] suspension of judgement naturally follows. How life can possibly be lived on such a basis is a question that will concern us in Chapter Five.

How accurately Sextus' scepticism reflects its Pyrrhonian original is indeed controversial. Pyrrho is recorded as saying that things are 'indifferent, unmeasurable and undecidable' (Aristocles, cited by Eusebius *Preparation for the Gospel* 14.18.3 = LS 1F), and that suspension of judgement will lead to tranquillity (*ataraxia*;

more on this in Chapter Five). The question arises whether the unknowability of external reality is due to limitations in us, or to its own nature. It seems likely that Pyrrho took the latter view; the very nature of external things is such as to be indeterminable, by contrast with the view of later 'Pyrrhonists' who stress rather the difficulty of achieving certainty and the lack of an agreed criterion.[21]

The history, and even the continuity, of the Pyrrhonian tradition between Pyrrho and Timon in the fourth and third centuries BC and the revival of Pyrrhonism in the first century BC is obscure. The first major figure of the revival is Aenesidemus, who classified considerations leading to suspension of judgement into ten 'modes', appealing successively (though the ordering is explicitly said to be an undogmatic one) to the different experiences of different creatures, different human beings, and so on. (Sextus, *PH* 1.36–7 = LS 72A; DL 9.79ff.; see further pp. 31–2). Subsequently Agrippa, whose very date is quite uncertain, distinguished five modes at a more general level; they included recognition of disagreement and of relativity (under which two Aenesidemus' ten modes can be subsumed), infinite regress, making assumptions, and circular argument (Sextus, *PH* 1.164ff., DL 9.88–9).

Sextus tells us that experience shows that there are equally strong arguments on both sides of every question ('equipollence'), so that we are led to suspend judgement. But whereas the Pyrrhonian sceptics report their Academic counterparts as holding just one dogmatic belief, the belief that one should not have any dogmatic beliefs (cf. e.g. Sextus, *PH* 1.3, also 1.233 = LS 68I; similarly Aenesidemus cited by Photius, *Library* 212 169b36ff. = LS 71C),[22] Sextus the neo-Pyrrhonian sceptic claims to escape even this. Scepticism for him is not an assertion that we should not have any beliefs, but simply a report of what happens to us when we try to arrive at the truth but find that we cannot (*PH* 1.15). It is like what happened to the painter Apelles who failed to paint the foam of a horse when he tried to, but succeeded in reproducing it when, in a fit of temper, he threw at the painting the sponge he used to wipe his brush on (*PH* 1.28). 'Sceptic' literally means 'inquirer'; paradoxically, it is their eagerness to find the truth that leads Sceptics to suspend judgement about it:

And for this reason, perhaps, in the case of the things searched for in philosophy, too, some say that they have found the truth, others have declared that it is not possible for this to be apprehended, while others are still searching. Those who think that they have found it are those properly called 'Dogmatists', for example the followers of Aristotle and Epicurus and the Stoics and certain others; declarations about it as inapprehensible have been made by the followers of Clitomachus and Carneades and other Academics; and the Sceptics are searching.

(Sextus, *PH* 1.2–3)

Suspension of judgement is an 'end' not in the sense of a goal but simply as where we end up[23] – or have done so far. For the Sceptic does not assert that evidence against scepticism itself will never turn up; rather, sceptical suspension of judgement 'is a sort of condition supervenient on continuous mild investigation' which involves no anxiety.[24] Nor should the Sceptic be thought of as weighing up arguments on each side of the question and constructing a case for suspension of judgement; the Sceptic does not arrive at a conclusion, but undergoes an experience.[25]

Hankinson argues that this absolves Sextus from the charge brought against him by Burnyeat, that of in effect trying both to eat his cake and to have it. Burnyeat argues that Sextus makes an illegitimate extrapolation from sense-experience; while I can report that some soup, say, seems too salty to me without committing myself to the view that it really is very salty, this no longer applies when it is a question of one's own thoughts. To say that something appears so to oneself without one's having an opinion about it is, Burnyeat argues, to treat 'it appears to me' and 'I think that it is' as distinct in a way in which they can be in the case of appearances to the senses, but cannot be where the 'appearing' is itself a matter of thinking.[26] Against this, however, Hankinson argues that Sextus is not committing himself to any judgement that there are in fact equally strong arguments on both sides of the question, but simply reporting his experience up till now.[27]

This explains another feature of neo-Pyrrhonist scepticism which may seem puzzling. The Aenesideman modes leading to suspension of judgement do not all seem equally persuasive; that things appear different to different animals (Sextus, *PH* 1.40–61 = LS 72B) may not seem as relevant to *human* uncertainty as the disagreements between Platonists and Epicureans (Sextus, *PH* 1.88 = LS 72C). Not everyone will accept that the experiences of the healthy are not to be privileged over those of the sick (Sextus, *PH* 1.101–3 = LS 72E); and the examples of optical illusions in Sextus, *PH* 1.118ff. = LS 72F include some of the very ones that are explained by Lucretius (4.426ff.). But equal persuasiveness is not, Hankinson argues, the point. The Sceptic is not presenting an organised case but putting forward every consideration that might lead to suspension of judgement; which ones do so in any particular case, and indeed whether *any* of them do, is not his concern, for he is telling us why we might feel doubt rather than seeking to prove a point. Again, while there has been much debate over whether Sextus' scepticism is 'rustic', involving suspension of judgement about the basis of everyday experiences, or 'urbane', directed against philosophical theories as Academic scepticism was, the truth seems to be that no decision on this question is needed; the Sceptic searches for the truth as and when perplexity arises, whatever the context, and finds that he is always led to suspension of judgement.

3

WHAT IS REALITY?

MATERIALISM OR CORPOREALISM

As in theory of knowledge, so in physics the Epicurean and Stoic systems are both similar and different. They have in common a belief that reality is, in broad terms, to be identified with what is bodily or corporeal – with material reality as we might say, though the associations of that term are likely to be misleading especially where the Stoics are concerned. The two schools share the same basic argument for restricting reality to bodies, and the same philo-sophical problems that 'materialism' brings, above all those of accounting for mind and consciousness (though this is more true of the Epicureans than of the Stoics, for reasons that we shall see). But the accounts they give of the nature of body are in certain respects diametrically opposed to one another. (The Sceptics will not figure in the present chapter at all – naturally enough, given that the Academic sceptics had no definite views on such matters, and the Pyrrhonian sceptics claimed to have no views on anything at all.)

The Stoics and Epicureans both in effect take an anti-corporealist argument of Plato's (whatever the actual historical connection may be) and turn it around. Plato consistently opposed materialism, arguing that soul must be prior to body rather than a product of it.[1] In the *Sophist*, claiming that both the corporeal and the incor-poreal must have a place in reality, he proposes that being real should be identified in terms not of being bodily but of possessing a capacity to affect other things or to be affected by them (247E) – so that not only soul but also justice and wisdom will, for Plato, be real though not bodily (247B). The Stoics and the Epicureans stood this argument on its head, arguing that since only what is bodily *can* have any effects, everything that does so – soul included – must be regarded as corporeal:

> Nothing can act or be acted on without body, and nothing can provide a place [for action] except what is void and empty.
>
> (Lucretius, 1.443 = LS 5B)

> [Zeno the Stoic] differed from [the Peripatetics and Academics] in that he thought that nothing could be brought about in any way by such a nature as was without body ... neither that which brought something about, nor that which was affected, could be other than a body.
>
> (Cicero, *Academica Posteriora* 1.39 = LS 45A)

One difference between the two schools' accounts of body, however, is already indicated in these arguments. The Epicurean text makes explicit reference to void; for Epicurus as for earlier atomists, as already indicated in Chapter Two, void must exist if movement is to be possible, and void carries with it the implication that body is made up of discrete particles. For the Stoics, on the other hand, matter or body is continuous, and there is no void within the one existing world (though there has to be void, indefinite rather than infinite in extent, outside it; for periodically the whole world is turned to fire, as we shall see, and it needs space into which to expand at those times, fire taking up more space than other stuffs).

EPICURUS

The Epicurean argument for the atomic structure of matter follows a similar sequence both in the *Letter to Herodotus* and in Lucretius. In both texts the starting point is the claim (*ad Hdt.* 38 = LS 4A; Lucretius, 1.149ff. = [in part] LS 4B) that nothing can come from nothing; only certain sorts of fruit can come from certain trees, and this must be because the right kind of 'seeds' are needed. ('Seeds' is explicitly – Lucretius, 1.59 – used as a general term for atoms; it is not confined to an initial starting point as contrasted with what is later added to it.) The idea of a regularity in natural coming-to-be is central to Lucretius, especially in connection with the idea that all compound bodies, including world-systems themselves, have a fixed and determinate lifespan;[2] and there is good reason to think that the argument from the regularity of nature goes back to the early atomists.[3]

A distinction does, however, need to be drawn which Epicurus and Lucretius do not make explicit. It is one thing to say (A) that nothing can come from nothing, in the sense that everything comes from *something* else that precedes it; another to say (B) that only certain things can come from certain things.[4] (A), the 'principle of conservation of matter', was universally accepted in ancient Greek thought at least from the time of Parmenides onwards. (B), too, is a matter of common experience. But just for that reason it is clear that both (A) and (B) were held by many to be compatible with theories other than atomism. For Aristotle the fact that some matter is a human being is due to the presence in it of the form of human being transmitted from the parent, and the matter's being of a certain sort is *explained by* its being matter for a human being, rather than vice versa; and for the Stoics matter was a continuum and in itself completely formless. In indicating that regularity in nature is to be explained by the presence of seeds of particular shapes and sizes the Epicureans are in effect denying the Aristotelian distinction between form and matter, or perhaps better, supposing that matter is *inherently* formed – matter exists simply, and only, as particles of certain sizes and shapes, even though the formal argument for the atomic, indivisible and unalterable nature of these particles is yet to come.

From the Atomist perspective, therefore, the distinction between (A) and (B) is an unreal one; a fruit of a particular type not only needs to be made of *some* matter, it needs to be made of particular sorts of atoms,[5] and any atom is inherently matter of a particular sort – i.e. a particle of a particular shape and size (for the stuff of which atoms are made is not different from one type of atom to another). Epicurus and Lucretius are not indeed guilty of assuming here what they are still in the first stage of setting out to prove; the atomic nature of the seeds of which they speak is still to be argued for, and the argument for it does not *rest* on the assertion of (B) rather than of (A). Nevertheless, in not distinguishing between (A) and (B) they are conducting their exposition in the perspective of their own system as a whole. And this is characteristic.[6]

The argument that the 'seeds' in question are indeed indivisible – *atoma*, atoms – comes later (*ad Hdt.* 41 = LS 8A; Lucretius, 1.485ff. = [in part] LS 8B), and rests first of all on the mutual exclusivity of body and void. Void must exist to allow for move-ment; if void and body both exist there must be some particles of body small enough to contain no void, and, it is argued, if these contain no void they will be physically indivisible, and so unalter-able. Second, indivisible particles not themselves subject to change are needed if all things are not to perish; Lucretius attacks rival theories (1.635–920) for making the first beginnings of things *weak* (and also for arbitrariness in selecting some sensible things as fundamental;[7] for the Atomists the fundamental particles are not like *any* sensible things).

There is, however, a further reason for postulating the existence of indivisible minima, inherited by Epicurus from the earlier atom-ists and – if we make a distinction which the earlier atomists themselves apparently did not – mathematical rather than physical in character. For the atomism of Leucippus and Democritus was in part a reaction to the paradoxes of Zeno of Elea (born c.490 BC; to be distinguished from Zeno of Citium, the founder of Stoicism); and some of these turn, explicitly or implicitly, on issues to do with repeated division. If a finite length can be divided into an infinite number of parts, each of those parts must have some size if the whole is to have any, but – Zeno wrongly supposed – an infinite number of parts each of which has size will produce an infinite, not a finite length, and thus contradict the original assumption (KRS 316). The best-known of Zeno's paradoxes, that of swift-footed Achilles and the tortoise (KRS 322) implicitly turns on the same point: if Achilles gives the tortoise a start in the race, then by the time he gets to where the tortoise started the tortoise will have moved on a bit, and by the time Achilles gets *there* the tortoise will have moved on a bit, and.... Or, more simply, you can never run the length of the stadium, because you always have half the remaining distance to go first (KRS 318). Both in these cases and in the one with which we started what is obviously finite – the finite length, the distance to the end of the stadium or to the point where we can in fact calculate Achilles will overtake the tortoise, given the size of the start and their respective speeds – turns out to be worryingly infinite. One possible answer to Zeno's paradoxes, the one which the atomists took, is to suppose that lengths, and therefore bodies, are not infinitely divisible: they are composed of a finite number of parts each with a minute, but finite size.

Leucippus and Democritus probably did not distinguish

between physical divisibility and being divisible in thought. But Epicurus did so, probably for the very good reason that if atoms are to have shapes, and indeed differing shapes, they must be divisible in thought though not physically. A spherical atom will have a diameter divided by its centre, for example. Nevertheless, Epicurus still held that there was a lower limit to divisibility even in thought; an atom, itself physically indivisible, can be divided in thought into a number of 'minimal parts', but these themselves are in turn finite in number in any given atom. That they are so was argued by Epicurus precisely on the grounds of the need to counter Zeno's paradox (though without naming him; *ad Hdt*. 57 = LS 9A); he also pointed out that the claim was not contradicted by our experience, for, just as with sight there comes a point where a distance is so small that when we think we are looking at one half of it we have in fact transferred our attention to the adjacent minimum visible extension (in modern jargon, the resolving power of our vision is limited), so, when we think we are dividing a minimum thinkable extension, we are in fact thinking of the adjacent one (*ad Hdt*. 58–9 = LS 9A; Lucretius, 1.599ff. = LS 9C). The argument by analogy from things seen to those unseen is characteristic.

If one asks how adjacent minima are related to one another, they cannot have their edges in contact, because being indivisible they cannot have edges at all (if they did, there would be a midpoint between them). Nor of course can they be in the same place: so, like the minimum sensibles described as analogous to them in *ad Hdt*. 58, they must 'measure magnitudes by means of their own peculiar characteristics'. (It also follows that we cannot sensibly ask what shape a minimal part is.) The doctrine of minimal parts may serve to explain why Epicurus held that the number of different shapes of atoms is not infinite (though it is very large; and the number of individual atoms of each shape is infinite).[8] For, if atoms are made up of minimal parts, the number of shapes that can result from different arrangements of a given number of parts is limited; an infinite number of shapes could only come about if more and more parts are added ('made up' and 'added', of course, with reference to our analysis, not to any actual physical process; the structure of each atom is fixed and minimal parts cannot *actually* be combined or separated, as Epicurus takes pains to point out). This may explain an odd report (KRS 561; contrast Epicurus' position in *ad Hdt*. 55–6 = LS 12A) that Democritus had said there could be an individual atom as large as a world; it may be not that Democritus actually asserted this (though he *might* have done so, on the grounds that there was no reason why it shouldn't be so), but that Epicurus argued that he was in fact committed to it as the natural consequence of a claim that the number of different shapes of atoms is infinite, coupled with Epicurus' own denial of infinite divisibility in thought.

The only permanent properties that atoms have are shape, weight and size (*ad Hdt.* 54 = LS 12D: and, since all atoms are made of the same stuff, weight is presumably proportional to size). If one asks what the stuff is of which atoms are made, there is nothing one can say about it in terms familiar to our experience, except perhaps that it is utterly unyielding; atoms cannot have properties such as colour or differences in texture or fluidity, which are rather the properties of combinations or compounds of atoms. They result, indeed, from the shape and arrangement of the underlying atoms; lead, for example, is heavier than wool because it contains less void (Lucretius, 1.358ff. = LS 6A), oil is more viscous than wine because its particles are more entangled and wormwood tastes less pleasant than honey because its atoms[9] are less smooth (Lucretius, 2.391ff. = LS 12F). (One should not, however, suppose that this means that for Epicurus compounds and their properties are in any sense less real than the underlying atoms; this issue has already been touched upon in connection with sensation in Chapter Two, and one aspect of it will be prominent in Chapter Four.) Atoms can, however, have attributes that apply to them temporarily, such as being in a particular position or orientation. And for compounds of atoms too there are both properties which are as permanent as this particular compound is (e.g. the heat of a fire, the fluidity of a quantity of water) and more temporary attributes (such as slavery or riches, for a human being). None of these properties or temporary attributes, however, exist in their own right; the only things that exist are bodies – i.e. the atoms and the compounds they go to make up – and the void that separates them.

For Epicurus, as for Democritus, atoms are constantly moving, colliding and rebounding in the void, making up, if they are of suitable types, compounds which last for a time and are then broken up. Even our world, with its planets and stars, is simply a compound of this sort; the universe as a whole is infinite both in time and space (for what could there be outside it?).[10] World-systems come to be within it, are maintained for a time by taking in atoms to replace those that are thrown off, and eventually break up. This much was doctrine shared by Epicurus and the earlier atomists; but Epicurus modified Democritus' account of atomic motion in two respects, probably in both cases in response to objections from Aristotle.

First, Democritus had apparently held that when atoms combine to form a body such as a book, a table or a tree, they cease to move independently and remain entangled together; if I move the book across the table, the only movement the atoms in it have is that of the book as a whole. But for Epicurus all atoms, whether currently in a compound body or not, are constantly moving with a speed described as 'fast as thought'; the atoms in the book or the table are vibrating just as fast as those in the air, and the appearance of stability is simply the result of their changing their course, due to collisions within the compound, much more frequently. Possibly this change in the theory was a reaction to Aristotle's pointing out that the view that there are indivisible minimum lengths is incompatible with things' moving at different speeds, since in the time that a faster thing takes to cover an indivisible length a slower one will only have covered part of an indivisible minimum length, which is a contradiction in terms (Aristotle, *Physics* 6.2 233b19ff.). Epicurus may have sought to

Figure 1

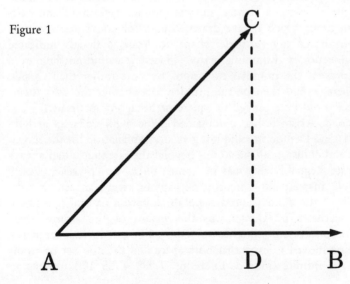

answer this by asserting that in fact all atoms move at the same speed (cf. LS pp. 51–2).

This will not, indeed, solve the problem if atoms can move at an angle to one another – if two atoms travel at the same speed but one due east and another at an angle of 45° to this, then in the time that the first atom takes to cover an indivisible minimum distance (AB in Figure 1) the second will cover the same distance (AC) in a north-easterly direction, but only part of an indivisible minimum, AD, if measured in an easterly direction.[11]

This problem can in turn be answered if not only bodies and space, but also time is composed of indivisible minima, so that atoms do not move continuously but proceed in staccato jerks, being first at one position and then at the next one but never in motion between them. The presence in atoms of minimal parts indivisible, even in thought, in any case carries with it the implication of staccato movement, as otherwise an indivisible minimal part would, in the movement of the atom it goes to make up, have only half of itself outside its former position before the whole was outside, and that again is a contradiction in terms. There is indeed evidence that Epicurus eventually adopted the view that bodies, space and time are all composed of indivisible minima (LS pp. 51–2). The movement through space of an atom with four minimal parts will then be something like that shown in Figure 2, though the number of minimal parts in most atoms is no doubt thought of as much greater, and the minimal extensions and parts within them which I have drawn square for convenience cannot actually be of any *particular* shape, for reasons already indicated in connection with minimal parts. (Indeed, it would not help even to represent the minimal extensions by dots rather than shapes; for there would then be the problem of whether the dots themselves should be arranged in square or hexagonal patterns.)

Second, Aristotle had complained (*Physics* 8.1 252a32; cf. KRS p. 424) that Democritus did not give any explanation for the movement and collision of the atoms, beyond the fact that it had always been so. Arguably that was in atomist terms the correct and only possible answer; but Epicurus, perhaps unwisely, argued that the weight of the atoms caused them all to have a natural movement downwards. (For Democritus the weight of the atoms seems simply to have amounted to something like our inertia, resistance to being moved.) Given that both space and the number of atoms in it are infinite (indeed, Lucretius, 1.988 = LS 10B uses as an

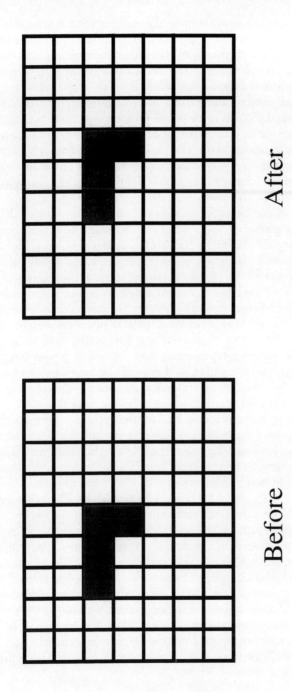

After

Before

Figure 2

argument for space being infinite the claim that, if it were not, all the atoms would end up at the bottom), it is not clear quite what sense can be given to the claim that we and everything else in the universe are all falling endlessly downwards (relative to what?),[12] quite apart from the question whether it makes any sense to regard one particular direction in infinite space as downwards rather than another.[13] But Epicurus nonetheless claimed that there was such a natural downwards movement of the atoms. Moreover, where it might be thought that, with all atoms naturally falling downwards, collisions would start when the heavier ones fell faster and overtook the lighter,[14] Epicurus argued – rightly – that in a vacuum all bodies, whatever their weight, fall at the same speed; apparent differences in the speed with which bodies visible to us fall are due to their greater or lesser ability to overcome the resistance of the air (Lucretius, 2.225ff. = LS 11H; cf. *ad Hdt.* 47, 61 = LS 11D, E). 'In a vacuum' in Epicurean terms amounts to saying 'where there are no collisions with other atoms to slow them down', and *ex hypothesi* we are considering the situation before any collisions start. However, before Epicurus is given too much credit for anticipating Galileo, we may note, first, that as just indicated he may have other, mathematical reasons too for saying that all atoms move at the same speed; second, that the claim applies only to atoms, not to the compound bodies made up of them; and third, that there is no question of uniform acceleration – the atoms move constantly at the same speed which is 'as quick as thought'.

If collisions between atoms are not the result of differing rates of fall, they must begin in some other way; and this is one of the two contexts in which Epicurus introduced the claim that falling bodies may deviate very slightly from their straight paths, sense-experience not being able to show that *no* such deviations occur (Lucretius, 2.249f. = LS 11H; see Chapter Two). There has been much discussion over whether the introduction of the swerve was primarily motivated by this cosmogonical requirement or by its use to defend human free will, to be discussed in Chapter Four. The state of our evidence makes it difficult to decide, but it may be remarked that, if we ask when the swerve that started the process of atomic collision and rebounding in the cosmos as a whole occurred, the answer, if the question is well put at all, would have to be 'an infinitely long time ago'. For if there was in fact a first swerve and it happened only a finite length of time ago, its effects could only have spread to a finite part of the infinite universe. That suggests that the notion of a 'first swerve' is a purely theoretical one. In fact, though, the use of the swerve to explain human free will suggests that swerves occur frequently both inside and outside of human souls, and it would offend against the principle of equilibrium (see Chapter Two) to suppose that this had not always been the case. This implies even more forcefully that the existence of a first swerve that started off the process of collision is a theoretical postulate rather than a historical claim;[15] though this may not exclude its having been the initial context in which the swerve was postulated.

THE STOICS

For the Stoics, as for the Epicureans, all reality is bodily. Everything in the universe – for them a single world-system – is produced by the action of the active principle, God, on the passive principle, matter; the latter is itself without any determining qualities and inert. If they are to act, in the one case, and be acted on, in the other, both principles must be bodily; so that for the Stoics there can be two bodies in the same place – indeed in every place (cf. LS 48). The active principle is present in each thing, causing it to be what it is:

> They consider that there are two principles of the whole of things, the active and the passive. The passive is quality-less substance, that is, matter, the active is the reason in it, that is God. This is eternal and, through the whole of matter, fashions each thing .... God and Mind and Fate and Zeus are one; and he has many other names in addition.
> (DL 7.134f. = LS 44B)

> ... they say that there are two principles of all things, God and matter, of which one is active and the other passive; and they say that God is mixed with matter, traversing it throughout and shaping and forming it and producing the universe in this way.
> (Alexander of Aphrodisias, *On Mixture* 224.33 = LS 45H)

This Stoic pantheism influenced Virgil:

> For indeed God permeates all the lands and the expanses of the sea and the lofty heaven; from him flocks and herds, men

and every kind of wild beast, everything when it is born
derives its delicate life: and to him indeed all things return
again when they are broken up, and Death has no place, but
living still they fly up to increase the number of the stars
and rise up to the high heaven.

(*Georgic* 4.221–7)

First of all the heaven and the earth and the expanses of the
sea and the shining globe of the moon and the Titan stars
are nourished by a spirit from within, and Mind, penetrating
every limb, moves the whole mass and is mingled with the
vast body. From this come the race of humans and that of
animals, and the flying birds, and the monsters which the
deep brings forth beneath its shining surface.

(*Aeneid* 6.724–9)

It also more recently influenced Wordsworth, not only in the well-
known lines

And I have felt
A presence that disturbs me with the joy
Of elevated thoughts, a sense sublime
Of something far more deeply interfused,
Whose dwelling is the light of setting suns,
And the round ocean and the living air,
And the blue sky, and in the mind of man:
A motion and a spirit, that impels
All thinking things, all objects of all thought,
And rolls through all things.

(Wordsworth, *Lines Composed a Few Miles
above Tintern Abbey*, 93–102)

but also and more definitely in the following, where the italicised
phrases involve distinctively Stoic terminology, as we shall see:

To every Form of being is assigned . . .
An *active Principle*: howe'er removed
From sense and observation, it subsists
In all things, in all natures: in the stars
Of azure heaven, the unenduring clouds,
In flower and tree, in every pebbly stone
That paves the brooks, the stationary rocks,
The moving waters, and the invisible air . . .

Spirit that knows no insulated spot,
No chasm, no solitude, from *link to link*
It circulates, the soul of all the worlds.
This is the *freedom* of the universe
Unfolded still the more, more visible,
The more we know; and yet is reverenced least,
And least respected in the human Mind,
Its most apparent home.
(Wordsworth, *The Excursion*, 9.1–20)[16]

For Zeno, the founder of the Stoic school, God was identified with fire: not the destructive fire that burns on our hearths but 'crafting fire' found principally in the heavens (Stobaeus, *Selections* 1.25.5, p. 213.15 Wachsmuth–Hense = LS 46D). For Chrysippus God's presence in earthly things is in the form of *pneuma*, breath or spirit, a fiery form of air.[17] *Pneuma* is present in living creatures as soul, in plants as 'nature' (*phusis*, with etymological overtones of 'growth'), and in lifeless things such as rocks and pieces of timber as *hexis* or 'constitution' (the Greek word is etymologically connected with the 'holding' or maintaining of things in a certain state). However, the situation is more complex. In living creatures the bones have *hexis*, and plant-like parts, such as nails and hair and the nutritive functions which animals share with plants, are due to 'nature'.[18]

Pneuma is capable of simultaneous movement outwards (probably due to the fire) and inwards (probably due to the air),[19] and the resulting 'tension' (an idea deriving, like much else in Stoicism, from the Presocratic philosopher Heraclitus) is used to explain phenomena as diverse as the mechanism of sight (see Chapter Two) and the intellectual and hence moral condition of a person's soul. Heraclitus indeed played for the Stoics something of the role that the earlier atomists did for Epicurus, except that the Stoics, and especially Chrysippus, sought support for their views also from interpretations of a wide range of earlier Greek thought and literature, while Epicurus rejected cultural traditions generally and did not accept even the views of the earlier atomists without explicit criticism.

For the Stoics God is present in the whole universe; indeed, since he gives every part of it the character it has, in a sense he *is* the universe. But he is present, as we have seen, in different parts of it in different ways. The fact that the universe as a whole is a rational living being does not mean that every part of it must be

45

so; and God can be present in all of it, not just in rational creatures, just as you as a whole can be rational without your fingers or feet being so.[20] Indeed, just as your soul has a 'ruling principle' (located in your chest, as we will see in Chapter Four), so there is a ruling principle of the whole world, with which God or Zeus can be identified in a primary way even though in another he is the whole world. And God controls the whole world, as the ruling part of your soul controls your body. Chrysippus placed the ruling principle of the world in the heavens; Cleanthes specifically in the sun (DL 7.139 = LS 47O).

Where for Epicurus matter is divided into discrete particles, for the Stoics it is continuous. Empty space exists only outside the (finite) universe, not within it. To the question whether the two circular faces produced by slicing through a cone are different in size (in which case the cone would have been not smooth but made up of a series of steps) or the same in size (in which case, if the answer is the same at every possible position, the cone will have been not a cone at all but a cylinder), an atomist would have no hesitation in answering that the two faces are different in size (and that, given the existence of indivisible minima, the cone *cannot* in fact be sliced at every point). Chrysippus answered for the Stoics that the two faces are neither the same size nor different in size, which sounds like an evasion but may be a way of saying, correctly on a continuum theory, that they are infinitesimally different (Plutarch, *CN* 1079E = LS 50C).

For the Stoics individual things such as people and tables are not just individual things but parts of a greater whole. Where Aristotle had distinguished between substances (roughly, clearly defined and independently existing individual things) on the one hand, and the qualities present in them on the other, the Stoics regarded individual things as qualitative modifications of the underlying combination of the active and passive principles. That combination is described as 'what underlies'; it was the first of the four Stoic 'categories' or 'genera'.[21] The second category comprises things such as people or animals, not quali*ties* but 'quali*fieds*' (*poia*), body qualified in a certain way. Third come 'dispositions' of those 'qualifieds', or rather those qualifieds 'disposed in some way' (*pôs echonta*) – that is, further, secondary features, such as knowledge. Fourth are things 'relatively so disposed' (*pros ti pôs echonta*), that is, for example, one person as being on the right of another or the father of another (the point being that such dispositions can change without any change in the thing itself that possesses them; A can change from being on the right of B to being on the left if B moves, even though A itself remains still, and – according to Simplicius, *On Aristotle's* Categories 166.15ff. = LS 29C – you similarly cease to be a father if your son dies). The use of adjectival forms for the 'categories', rather than noun forms, is significant; when the Stoics insisted that 'qualities were bodies', or rather that 'qualifieds were bodies' (Simplicius, *On Aristotle's* Categories 217.32, cf. 271.20 = LS 28L, 28K), they meant not that your virtue was another separate body inside your body, but that virtue is always a condition of someone's (corporeal) soul, not an abstract or incorporeal entity. (Actually there was debate – cf. LS p. 177 – over whether the moral state of an individual's soul, being so fundamental to it in the Stoic view, belonged in 'category' two or rather in 'category' three, but that does not affect the general point.)

What is *in*corporeal 'subsists' (*huphistasthai*) but does not exist (*einai*) – this class including *lekta*, the meanings of (some) words (see Chapter Two), place, time and the void outside the world (Sextus, *M* 10.218 = LS 27D). 'Qualifieds' are divided into 'individually qualifieds' (such as individual human beings) and 'commonly qualifieds' (such as human beings in general). The 'commonly qualifieds', we are told, are primary (Syrianus, *On Aristotle's* Metaphysics 28.18 = LS 28G); since only individuals exist, and universal notions like that of human being in general are mental constructs, the implication, if indeed this text is to be trusted, must be that the Stoics share with Aristotle the view that each individual human being is *primarily* a human being – characterised by the features that are common to human beings in general – and only secondarily an individual in the sense of having individual peculiarities. The Stoics certainly cannot be committed to anything like separately existing Platonic universals, the transcendent Forms of Human Being and Table and the like. Indeed for the Stoics a statement such as 'a human being is a rational mortal animal' is to be interpreted as 'if anything is a human being, it is a rational mortal animal' (Sextus, *M* 11.8 = LS 30I). The treatment of 'this person is sitting' as definite while 'Socrates is sitting' is intermediate (Sextus, *M* 8.97 = LS 34H) can hardly suggest that Socrates as an individual with a life-history is secondary to the succession of individual Socrateses who sit and walk in particular places at particular times – the Stoics clearly regard the unity of the individual, while he survives, as more fundamental than *that*; nevertheless, it may serve to highlight the Stoic emphasis on individual bodily existents, seen always as configurations of particular parts of the totality of being, the universe.

First among the determinations of matter by the active principle are the four 'elements', fire, air, water and earth (DL 7.136–7 = LS 46B, 47B; Stobaeus, *Ecl.* 1.10.16, p. 129.2ff. Wachsmuth–Hense = LS 47A). There may seem to be a paradox in the four elements being produced by an interaction of the two principles when one of the principles is itself fire (for Zeno) or fire and air (for Chrysippus); but the paradox can be resolved by supposing that, since the two principles never exist apart from one another, fire is that condition of the two principles together which is most divine. The fact that we have fire rather than (say) water will after all depend entirely on the active principle, the passive being inert and itself contributing nothing beyond its simple existence.

Periodically the whole world turns to fire, in a 'conflagration' (*ekpurôsis*) which is not so much a destruction as an apotheosis: the whole world becomes, in the fullest sense, God or Zeus. (Plutarch, *SR* 1052C, 1053B = LS 46EF. The other traditional Greek gods were regarded by the Stoics as different aspects or names of this single divinity; DL 7.147 = LS 54A.) Seneca (*Letters on Morals* 9.16 = LS 46O) uses Zeus' resting at this time as an analogy for a wise man's withdrawing into his own thoughts in time of misfortune; the idea of God withdrawing was already present in Plato (*Politicus* [Statesman] 272E; cf. *Timaeus* 42E) and recalls the Sphere of the Presocratic Empedocles (cf. KRS 358). Perhaps it is at this time that the Stoic God enjoys the tranquillity which, as we shall see below, the Epicurean gods always enjoy.

The fire then goes out (presumably because the moisture on which it feeds has all been used up),[22] and turns to water, but Zeus remains behind as a spark in the water containing in himself the 'seminal rational principles' (*spermatikoi logoi*) of all things in the future world ('Aëtius' 1.7.33, DL 7.135 = LS 46AB), which then develops in exactly the way it did before, history repeating itself in endless cycles (Nemesius, *On the Nature of Man* 38, p. 111.18ff. Morani = LS 52C). Some Stoics, apparently troubled by the question how, if history repeats itself exactly, one cycle can be said to be different from another, took the perhaps unwise step of saying that *some* things could be different – enough to differentiate one cycle from another, but not enough to make any real difference. For example, in one cycle a person might have a mole on his face, in another not (Alexander of Aphrodisias, *On Aristotle's* Prior Analytics 181.25 = LS 52F). Just as the Stoic world is a living creature, so it has a 'biological' life-cycle, growing and developing as a living creature would[23] (the fact that the growth and eventual transformation into fire of the universe is explained in terms of physical processes in no way conflicts with this, in Stoic terms, for there is no sharp division between the physical and the biological). Once again, for all the differences, there is a certain similarity between Stoic and Epicurean theories; for Epicurean world-systems in the infinite universe have their fixed life-cycles too.

The course of events is entirely predetermined, each given set of circumstances inevitably giving rise to one particular outcome: Alexander of Aphrodisias, *On Fate* 191.30ff. = LS 55N, especially 192.22ff.:

It is impossible that, when all the circumstances surrounding both the cause and that for which it is a cause are the same, the matter should sometimes not turn out in a particular way and sometimes should. For if this happens there will be some motion without a cause.

This formulation may be a later development, but from Chrysippus himself we have '(Fate is) a certain natural connected ordering of all things, one group of things following on and involved with another from eternity, such a weaving-together allowing no avoidance' (Chrysippus cited by Gellius, *Attic Nights* 7.2.3 = LS 55K). Nothing can happen without a cause:

Speaking against these people on the grounds that they violate nature by introducing what is without cause, Chrysippus in many places adduces the knucklebone and the balance, and many of the things that cannot [he says] fall or incline in different ways at different times without some cause and difference either concerning them or concerning what comes from outside. For what is uncaused and spontaneous is altogether non-existent; in the case of the adventitious impulses that are invented and spoken of by certain people undetected causes intrude, and we are not aware that they lead the impulse in one direction.

(Plutarch, *SR* 1045B)

This has been claimed[24] as anticipating the methodology of modern scientific enquiry; but as with Epicurean astronomy, so here the motivation was theological rather than scientific, and the Stoics were for the most part more concerned with asserting that the universe was a unified causal system than with pursuing investigations of the reasons for apparent discrepancies. (Posidonius, whose interest in investigating natural phenomena caused him to be described as 'Aristotelianising' – Strabo 2.3.8 = Posidonius T85 Edelstein–Kidd – is an exception here.)

The chain of causes, which is fate, is identified with providence and with Zeus (DL 7.135 = LS 46B; Cicero, *On the Nature of the Gods* 1.39 = LS 54B; Plutarch, *SR* 1056C = LS 55R) – reasonably enough, for Zeus is after all present in each thing, making it what it is and thus causing it to have the effects on other things that it does. Everything that happens is simply the inexorable unfolding of the plan present in Zeus at the start of each world-cycle. Thus, while the natural tendencies of individual things can be impeded, the nature of the whole cannot (Plutarch, *SR* 1056D); and the individual things are parts of that greater whole. The implications of this for ethics will concern us in subsequent chapters. We do indeed also find providence and fate described as God's *will* (Calcidius, *On Plato's* Timaeus 204 = LS 54U), which could suggest a hierarchical distinction between God and the world whose history he wills; but this is a late source, and when Chrysippus himself described fate as 'the rational account (*logos*) of the things in the world that are managed by providence' (Stobaeus, *Selections* 1.5.15, p. 79.1 Wachsmuth–Hense = LS 55M) he may not have intended any metaphysical distinction. Posidonius placed Zeus first, nature second and fate third ('Aëtius' 1.28.5 = Posidonius fr 103 EK).

The alleged effectiveness of divination by omens was used as an argument for the existence of the fated causal nexus (Diogenianus ap. Eusebius, *Preparation for the Gospel* 4.3.1 = LS 55P); the state of the sacrificial victim's entrails does not indeed *cause* the victorious outcome of the imminent battle, but it is linked with it, since all things are linked together in a single system (the doctrine of 'sympathy' or *sumpatheia*), though diviners have built up their art by observing the correlations rather than by understanding the unseen connections:

Moreover, since everything happens by fate ... if there could

be any mortal who could observe with his mind the intercon-
nection of all causes, nothing indeed would escape him. For
he who knows the causes of things that are to be necessarily
knows all the things that are going to be. But since no one
but God could do this, what is left for man is that he should
be aware of future things in advance by certain signs which
make clear what will follow. For the things which are going
to be do not come into existence suddenly, but the passage
of time is like the unwinding of a rope, producing nothing
new but unfolding what was there at first.

> (Cicero, *On Divination* 1.127 = LS 55O)

The Stoics do not think that God is concerned with individual fissures in livers or songs of birds – that would be
neither seemly nor worthy of the gods nor in any way able
to happen; rather, right from the start the universe began in
such a way that certain things are preceded by certain signs,
some in entrails, some in [the flight of] birds, some in lightning, some in portents, some in the stars, some in the visions
of dreamers, some in the utterances of the raving. Those who
have observed these things well are not often wrong; bad
conjectures and interpretations are false not through any
shortcoming in the things themselves, but because of the
ignorance of the interpreters.

> (ibid. 1.118 = LS 42E)

Even the gods' knowledge of the future seems to depend not so
much on their understanding of the workings of the world as on
the fact that, since history repeats itself, they have quite literally
seen it all before (Nemesius, *On the Nature of Man* 38, p. 111.25ff.
Morani = LS 52C). Panaetius doubted divination (Cicero, *On
Divination* 1.6) and rejected both astrology (ibid. 2.88) and the
periodic conflagration (Philo, *On the Eternity of the World* 76–7 =
LS 46P); the last had also been rejected by Boethus of Sidon,
fellow-pupil with Panaetius of Diogenes of Babylon, who had
himself suspended judgement on the issue (ibid.).

Because divination was thought to be based on observation of
regular conjunctions of portents and what they portended, rather
than on understanding of the true causes, Chrysippus argued that
its observations should be expressed in the form not of (e.g.) 'if
Fabius was born with the Dog-star rising, he will not die at sea',
but rather of 'not both: Fabius was born with the Dog-star rising

and Fabius will die at sea' (Cicero, *On Fate* 15–17 = [in part] LS 38E). It is not immediately clear how the formulation achieves anything in the context in which Cicero scornfully reports it, which is that of Chrysippus' attempt to argue that the fact that one outcome has been foretold does not mean that the alternative is *impossible*, even though everything is predetermined and divination is believed to derive its validity from that fact. To see what is at issue will involve something of a digression.

It might indeed seem that, if everything that happens is predetermined, nothing other than what actually happens is possible. But the Stoics did not take this view. It *had* indeed been held, probably on logical grounds rather than as an implication of physical determinism, by Diodorus Cronus (see Chapter Two), who held that only what is or will be true is possible (the past already being fixed, so that possibility is directed towards the future; the thought was presumably that it is inappropriate to say that something is 'possible' if we know that it happened once but will never happen again). Diodorus' pupil Philo went to the other extreme, saying that whatever was in accordance with the 'bare fitness', i.e. the nature, of the thing involved was possible, even if was prevented, so that it was possible for chaff at the bottom of the sea to be burned (Alexander of Aphrodisias, *On Aristotle's* Prior Analytics 183.34ff. = LS 38B). Chrysippus, however, regarded the possible as what admitted of being true *and* was not prevented (DL 7.75 = LS 38D), thus drawing the bounds of the possible more narrowly than Philo; but he also argued, against Diodorus, that some things that would not happen were still possible (Cicero, *On Fate* 13 = LS 38E).

Critics like Cicero replied that the Stoics could not, if they maintained their belief in determinism, say that things that did not happen were not prevented; they were surely prevented by the very factors that brought about the alternatives which *did* happen (so too Alexander of Aphrodisias, *On Fate* 176.14ff. = LS 38H). And indeed it is not immediately clear how Chrysippus could maintain the view he did. (*Why* he did so will concern us in Chapter Four.) It has been suggested that the Stoic view of possibility was an 'epistemic' one, that things that will not happen are possible for us because we do not *know* that they will in fact be prevented from doing so – the implication of that being, as Alexander points out (ibid.), that the same thing will be possible in some people's view and not in others'. But the evidence for this rests only on the one passage just cited from Alexander, who may here as elsewhere be more interested in developing his own argument than in reflecting Stoic views accurately, together with Simplicius, *On Aristotle's* Categories 196.2–4, who refers, without explicitly naming the Stoics, to the view that a thing is possible if there is no *obvious* impediment to it. In the latter case, however, it is not clear that obviousness is relative to particular observers or that its absence is what *constitutes* possibility (see LS vol. 2, p. 237).

Admittedly, there is a similarity between possibility defined in terms of our ignorance and the Stoic view of *chance*. In a providentially ordered universe there can be no such thing as chance, if that is regarded as what is essentially unplanned; and so the Stoics took over the view, already known to Aristotle (*Physics* 2.4 196b5), that chance is 'a cause obscure to human reason' (Simplicius, *On Aristotle's* Physics 333.1ff. = *SVF* 2.965; 'Aëtius' 1.29.7 = *SVF* 2.966). It is not, however, clear that the Stoic view of *possibility* must necessarily be similar. It may rather be that Chrysippus refused to accept that a future non-event could be described as 'prevented' now just because the course of destiny will eventually lead to its being prevented – especially perhaps when the only reason why something will not occur is that it is predetermined that we, the human agents, will not do it, and there is no *external* impediment.[25] (However, it is not clear that *all* cases of 'non-prevention' turn on the involvement of human agency; see below.)

It is in this context that the point of Chrysippus' formulation of the diviners' observations may become apparent. Fabius' having been born at the rising of the Dog-star does not *prevent* his dying at sea, it is simply that observation shows (allegedly) that the two things, being born at the rising of the Dog-star and dying at sea, do not go together. There must on Stoic principles be a reason for this, but (i) we do not know it, and (ii) – on the second interpretation of the Stoic doctrine of possibility, see above – it does not follow that we can speak of Fabius' dying at sea as being *prevented* (as we could if, for example, he had just died on land, or was on his death-bed a hundred miles from the sea, given the slow speed of ancient land-transport). True, the absence of prevention in this case may have little to do with the distinction between human agency and external impediment; but that particular contrast may not have been as central for the Stoics as it was for their anti-determinist critics.

If all things are governed by divine providence, the existence of evils needs to be explained. For the Stoics this task was in one way less severe than might at first be thought, since, as we shall see in Chapter Five, they regarded human wickedness as the only true evil. Cleanthes, indeed, argued that this was the one thing *not* governed by divine providence, though providence could turn it to good effect. Chrysippus did not follow him in this. And, although moral evil is the only true evil – and evil for the wrongdoer, not for the victim – Chrysippus did endeavour to explain both moral evil and other, apparent 'evils' in the world. Good could not exist if evil did not (Gellius, *Attic Nights* 7.1.2–6 = LS 54Q). But this can hardly explain why, in a divinely ordered world, almost all human beings were in the Stoic view bad, as we shall see in Chapter Five. Desirable consequences may have unfortunate side-effects, such as the thinness of the human skull which (it was said) aids our intelligence but brings with it fragility (Gellius, *Attic Nights* 7.1.7ff. = LS 54Q: the argument, and the example, being taken from Plato's *Timaeus*, 75BC). And apparent evils may have good consequences not immediately apparent to us; thus (quoting Euripides' *Helen*) the Trojan War was devised by the gods as a means of human population control (Plutarch, *SR* 1049B), lions exist to exercise our courage (Porphyry, *On Abstinence* 3.20.1 = LS 54P) and bed-bugs to discourage sloth (Plutarch, *SR* 1044D = LS 54O). Everything else in the world exists for the sake of gods and men; the only reason pigs have souls is to serve like salt, in keeping the meat fresh until we are ready to eat it. (Porphyry, loc. cit. The Academic sceptic Carneades objected that in that case pigs would be benefited by being slaughtered and eaten; no Stoic response is recorded, but it might well be that, while pigs would indeed be happy to become bacon if they knew what was truly good for them, even human beings do not, Stoic sages excepted, succeed in recognising their own best interests.) Both Stoic attempts to explain apparent evils and their positive arguments for providence – set out at great length in the second book of Cicero's *On the Nature of the Gods*, among other places – influenced the long subsequent history of attempts to 'justify the ways of God to men' (Milton, *Paradise Lost* 1.26). For example, providential design is shown in the placing of your eyebrows (above your eyes to stop sweat running into them) and your nose (above your mouth to enable you to assess the edibility of your food). (Cicero, *On the Nature of the Gods* 2.143, 2.140.)

However, where moral evil is concerned the Stoics, or at least those like Chrysippus who try to claim that divine providence governs everything, have greater problems. They need to explain the mechanism by which it comes about that, in a providentially ordered world, almost all people are bad (i.e. not Stoic sages). Chrysippus blamed what the majority of people say, and the persuasiveness of impressions (Galen, *PHP* 5.5.14ff., 19; part = LS 65M); Calcidius says that the Stoics held that the problem starts with nurses who give infants the misguided idea that being comfortable is good and being uncomfortable bad (Calcidius, *On Plato's* Timaeus, 165). But to blame the previous generation in every case simply pushes the problem back into the past; it does not solve it. Posidonius' introduction of a distinct and fundamentally irrational element in the human soul (on which more in Chapter Four) changes the terms of the problem (and was indeed intended to do so). But to introduce an irrational element into the human soul is one thing, to introduce it into the universe as a whole another. The tension in Posidonius' view is suggested, perhaps, by his definition of the goal of human life as 'To live contemplating the truth and order of the whole and joining in establishing it as far as possible, in no respect being led by the irrational part of the soul' (Clement, *Miscellanies* 2.21.129.4 = LS 63J), for it at once raises the question how the irrational part of the soul referred to in the last clause relates to the truth and order of the whole referred to in the first clause. Indeed John Rist has seen the disruption of the earlier Stoic view of the universe as the *effect* of Posidonius' innovations.[26]

Orthodox Stoics, who regard the world as a single providentially ordained system, need to explain not just *how* but *why* the world has been arranged in a way that involves so much wickedness. Moreover, preserving human responsibility, as we shall see in Chapter Four Chrysippus as well as Cleanthes claimed to do, causes a further difficulty; for if virtue or its absence is *our* responsibility, as we shall see in Chapter Four the Stoics held it to be, and if virtue alone is good, it turns out that the one thing that is good is the one thing that the beneficent and providential gods cannot actually give us – as critics gleefully observed (Plutarch, *SR* 1048CE; Alexander of Aphrodisias, *Questions and Solutions* 1.14 and 2.21, 70.2ff.).

EPICURUS ON THE GODS

The Epicurean view of the gods was diametrically opposed to the Stoic belief in providence. For Epicurus the gods exist, indeed, as the common opinion of mankind shows (*ad Men.* 123 = LS 23B; Cicero, *On the Nature of the Gods* 1.43–5 = LS 23E); but they have no concern for our world and its affairs. To suppose that they do would be incompatible with their divine happiness and tranquillity. The first of Epicurus' *Principal Doctrines* asserts that 'What is blessed and immortal neither has troubles itself nor causes them for another, and accordingly is not affected either by anger or favour; for everything like this is characteristic of what is weak.'

Our world and the things in it, for all their regularity, are the products of chance rather than design, and in particular they are not designed by divine agency. We see because we have eyes, rather than having eyes in order to see (Lucretius, 4.823ff. = LS 13E), and, in a famous passage, the child's crying when born bears witness to the evils of life ahead (id. 5.222ff. = LS 13F). Conventional religion destroys tranquillity because it is based on false fears of the gods derived from mental images apprehended both in waking and in dreams, and from observation of heavenly phenomena (id. 5.1161ff. = LS 23A). A right understanding of the gods, by contrast, will be beneficial to us because the gods, human in form, are the supreme example of that tranquillity to which the Epicurean aspires:

> Unless you cast all these things out from your mind and put far away thoughts that are unworthy of the gods and alien to their peace, the holy divinity of the gods which you yourself have weakened will often cause you to stumble; not because the high power of the gods can be violated, so that in anger they resolve to seek sharp penalties, but because, when you yourself suppose those who are tranquil in calm peace to be seething with great waves of anger, you will not approach the shrines of the gods with a calm heart, nor will you have strength to take in, with tranquil peace of mind, the images which are carried to the minds of men from the holy bodies, indicating their divine form.
>
> (Lucretius, 6.68ff. = LS 23D)

For many ancient critics Epicurus' recognition of the existence of gods at all was simply evidence that he did not have the courage of his convictions. To such critics there was no real difference between belief in gods who did not care for our world, on the one hand, and out-and-out atheism, on the other – and indeed Plato had already, before Epicurus, classed denial of divine providence, even among those who believed in the existence of gods, as a type of atheism.[27] However, as we have already seen in Chapter Two, Epicurus not only asserted the existence of gods but described the mechanism by which we are aware of them, atomic images acting directly on the mind. In some sources Epicurus' gods are described as dwelling in the *intermundia*, the spaces between world-systems in the infinite universe (id. 5.146ff. = LS 23L), and as being, apparently, only one atom thick – virtually two-dimensional images, therefore:

> The gods have the appearance of men. But that appearance is not body, but like body; nor does it contain blood, but something like blood . . . . the nature of the gods is such that, first, it is apprehended not by the senses but by the mind, and not in solidity or individuality, like those things which [Epicurus] because of their stability calls solids, but rather, when a succession of similar images are apprehended, since an endless series of very similar images arises from innumerable individuals and flows towards them, our mind with the greatest of pleasure concentrates on these images and fixes on them, and gains an understanding of what the nature is that is both blessed and eternal.
>
> (Cicero, *On the Nature of the Gods* 1.48ff. = LS 23E)

Cicero's Epicurean spokesman here puts the point negatively: the gods are not solid bodies, and they are apprehended by a stream of similar images – that much being true of all objects, so that the point is presumably that in the case of the gods this is *all* that there is. However, if, since atomic images are constantly streaming off from the gods, as from all atomic compounds, and since atoms are always being added to all compounds as long as they survive to make good the loss, the question arises why the god itself should be identified with any particular one-atom-thick slice of the constant image-stream rather than with any other. And that leaves open the possibility that the gods really have *no* substantial existence other than as the stream of images which we interpret; that Epicurus' gods exist in our minds at least as much as anywhere else.[28]

That might suggest that we simply construct the gods in our minds from images from other sources – much as we see centaurs in dreams when horse- and man-images combine. Indeed, the text of Cicero just quoted speaks of images flowing *towards* the gods, though this has often been emended to 'from the gods'. However, Epicurus is committed not only to the view that the stream of atomic images exists objectively, but also to the view that there are right and wrong notions about the nature of the gods in a way that there are no right notions about centaurs, except the notion that they cannot exist. The gods cannot therefore be simply arbitrary mental constructs; certain conceptions of the divine are correct, because logically consistent, and others, such as that they are concerned with affairs in our world, are inconsistent with their blessedness and therefore wrong. And, since the images of the gods accessible only to thought are, like other such images, present everywhere, Epicurus' doctrine will, surprisingly enough, if this interpretation is correct, turn out to assert the omnipresence of the divine as much as do the Stoics – the difference being that these gods are in the world (though affecting, presumably, only human minds) but have no concern for the world.

4

WHAT ARE WE?

SOUL AND BODY

Since both Epicureans and Stoics regarded bodies as the only real existing things, in accounting for human beings' self-consciousness and sense of personal identity they encountered the problems, still familiar to us, of the relation between mind and matter, between mind and body, and between the laws of physics and our sense of our own freedom of action. For the ancient Greeks questions about human functioning were questions relating not so much to the mind as to the 'soul' (*psuchê*). That term, if used at all nowadays, tends to indicate a spiritual self distinct both from mind and from body; but for the Greeks *psuchê*, which could denote simply 'life' or 'life-force', related to all the ways in which living things function which set them apart from inanimate objects – not only thought, characteristic of human beings, but also sensation and the apparent power of initiating their own movements. (The fact that we no longer talk about 'soul' in this way is due above all to Descartes, who wanted to draw a sharp line between reasoning, on the one hand, and the functions we share with the rest of the animals, on the other.)[1]

EPICURUS

For Epicurus the soul is an atomic structure extending throughout the rest of the body, but interwoven with it in such a way that neither body nor soul can survive without the other (Lucretius, 3.323ff). (Since soul itself is made up of atoms and therefore bodily, Epicurus uses the term 'flesh' to indicate the rest of the body apart from the soul.) At death the atoms that make up our soul survive

59

– as they must, since all atoms are indestructible; but the compound which they form, the soul, ceases to exist, and even if the very same atoms should come together and form a soul once more, as Lucretius holds in the infinity of time they may well do,[2] this will in no sense be the *same* soul, since continuity on the level of the compound will have been broken. No survival of the soul after death is possible, as Lucretius argues in a sequence of 29 arguments:[3] the fact that the soul, understood in terms of thought and consciousness, can be affected during life by injury, alcohol, sickness and old age shows its perishability, and it is inconceivable that consciousness should survive without sense-organs. Those with other conceptions of the nature and activity of the soul and the part it plays during bodily life will not find these arguments convincing, and will not see senility as an argument against immortality; but they will need to refine their account of the relation between soul and body in the light of Lucretius' arguments.

The soul extends throughout the body, but its central part, the seat of consciousness (called by Lucretius *animus* as opposed to *anima* for the whole soul, and conventionally translated by 'mind'), is located in the chest (not the head),[4] on the grounds that it is there that we feel emotions (Lucretius, 3.140ff. = LS 14B). The *anima* extended through the rest of the body functions somewhat in the way we now know the nervous system does (though not to be identified with it),[5] transmitting sensations from the rest of the body to the mind and impulses to movement from the mind to the limbs. The transmission of sensations and impulses, like the processes of thought and imagination in the mind themselves, are all to be understood in terms of arrangements and patterns of movement in the atoms that make up the soul; indeed we are told that the soul needs the rest of the body not just to hold it together but to enable it to perform the 'sense-giving movements', the patterns of atomic movement without which there is no sensation and so no life. Sensation is not, however, a property of the soul alone, but of the compound of body and soul (Epicurus, *ad Hdt.* 63–6 = LS 14A; Lucretius, 3.350ff.); to say that our soul looks out through our eyes as through doors (we would say 'through windows', but windows were not a prominent feature of ancient Greek and Roman houses) is to incur the objection, according to Lucretius, that we ought then to see better if our eyes were removed, just as we can see through a door better if the door-posts are removed (id. 3.367ff.). The point is important for Epicurus presumably because a soul that simply looked out through the eyes might be more likely to be thought capable of functioning without the body at all.

Both parts of the soul, *animus* and *anima* alike, are made up of four types of atom:[6] atoms like those of heat, atoms like those of wind or breath, atoms like those of air, and atoms of another, unnamed type, which are the finest and the first to be affected in sensation:

> And for this reason again and again one may know that the nature of the mind and the soul is created from very minute seeds, because when it departs it takes no weight away with it. We must not, however, think that this nature is simple; for a certain thin breath mixed with heat deserts the dying, and heat moreover draws air with it; for there is no heat that does not have air mixed with it. For since it is agreed that its nature is rare, necessarily many first beginnings of air move around within it. So now the nature of the mind has been found to be triple; however, all these things are not enough to create sensation, since the mind does not admit that any of these can create the movements of sensation and whatever the mind ponders. So it is necessary that a certain fourth nature should be added to these. This is altogether without a name; there is nothing more mobile or finer than this, nor anything made of smaller or smoother particles. It is this that first spreads the movements of sensation through the limbs, for it is first to be moved, being made up of small shapes. Then heat and invisible wind take up the movement, then air; then everything is set in motion, the blood is disturbed, then the entrails feel everything, and finally the pleasure, or opposite violent feeling, is transmitted to the bones and marrow.
>
> (Lucretius, 3.228ff.)

The proportion of the different soul-ingredients is correlated by Lucretius (3.294ff. = LS 14D) with different psychological characteristics – heat with anger, wind with fear, air with placidity; but, though we cannot completely change the characteristics we are born with, any human being can, by following Epicurean precepts, come to live a life worthy of the gods (Lucretius, 3.322 = LS 14D).

Here, however, we encounter a number of problems. First, it is not clear whether the atoms in the soul like those of heat, breath and air are those which in other contexts, outside the body, make up these substances as normally understood, or whether we are dealing with a separate type of atoms, which are like those making up these substances in their familiar form, but not identical with them. Lucretius' remark that 'a *certain* thin breath . . . deserts the dying' (3.232, cited on p. 61) may suggest that the breath you breathe out when you breathe your last and lose your soul is different in kind from ordinary breath; but the association of warmth and/or breath in the ordinary sense with soul, i.e. with life, goes back a long way in Greek thought, reflecting its start from the obvious facts that dead bodies are cold and do not breathe.

The atoms of the unnamed third or fourth type are smaller and more mobile than those of any other substance, and must be so, we are told, in order to explain the distinctive processes of consciousness and thought (Lucretius, 3.238ff., quoted on p. 61). In postulating these atoms of a special type Epicurus is not compromising his materialism as such, for the atoms of the unnamed type are, after all, *atoms*; like any other atoms they are material bodies, indestructible, and not themselves possessed of consciousness or indeed of any properties other than shape, size or weight. But even if Epicurus is not actually going against his own materialism, the postulation of the atoms of the third or fourth nature is problematic, in two ways.

First of all, these atoms are unique in that they cannot be related, even indirectly, to any substance or stuff in our experience, in the way that the other ingredients of the soul can; Epicurus is in effect postulating a special 'soul-material' (or, strictly, atoms which have a function in souls but none elsewhere) to explain the phenomena of consciousness. Atoms of the fourth, unnamed kind must be present in the world at large – both the principle of equilibrium and the dispersal of the atoms of an individual's soul at death require this; but they have no direct effect or significance detectable by us unless they are within a soul. This might be thought to be materialism, indeed, but materialism of a rather peculiar type. No doubt Epicurus' answer would be, first that the evidence of our senses compels us to postulate such a type of atoms, and second that he has, after all, inferred various features of these atoms – their smallness and mobility – from the evidence of the senses (together with certain assumptions about the way in which atoms of different sizes and shapes move), so that he is not simply making an empty postulate along the lines of Molière's medical exam-candidate whose admired explanation for the effects of opium is that it has a 'sleep-giving power' (*virtus dormativa: Le Malade imaginaire*, finale).

But the claim that the evident phenomena of consciousness compel the postulation of a special type of atoms is itself problematic. The whole point of the atomic theory, after all, is that different arrangements and combinations of atoms can produce different substances; Lucretius repeatedly illustrates this by the rearrangement of a limited range of letters in the alphabet to produce many different words, and even (1.914) illustrates the production of fire from logs of wood by the fact that the Latin words, *ignis* and *ligna*, have most of their letters the same. This is arguably not just a pun, but an illustration of the similar principles that operate throughout the universe; Lucretius' poem and the letters that go to make it up are *themselves* parts of the 'nature of things'. The illustration was an old one: Democritus had used differences in shape between letters, different positions of the same shape (Z and N) and different arrangements of letters to illustrate the formation of compounds from atoms (KRS 555), and Aristotle illustrates the theory of the early atomists by the fact that tragedies and comedies are made up of the same letters (Aristotle, *On Coming To Be and Passing Away* 1.1 315b14 = KRS 562). True, the change from *ligna* to *ignis*, and even the change in colour of the sea when waves break (Lucretius, 2.770 = LS 12E), involve not just rearrangement of the same atoms but some addition and subtraction of atoms – processes which are going on constantly anyway; but it is essential to the theory that atoms should not be identified as each being able to make up one and only one stuff on the level of our experience. (The metaphor of 'levels' is in effect Lucretius' own: 3.273, 284 = LS 14D.)

Moreover, Lucretius' account in book 2 of the properties possessed by compounds but not by atoms (2.730–1022; part in LS 12E) has as its climax the argument that animate beings can be made up of inanimate particles; if this were not so, we would have to suppose that the individual atoms of which we are made up could have a sense of humour and inquire into the composition of things and their own first principles (2.976ff. – one absurdity here being that they are themselves first principles and so do not have any further ones, unless we are to engage in the infinite regress that it was the aim of the atomic theory to prevent). There is no mention here of any special type of atom being needed; on the contrary, it is the particular arrangement of ingredients themselves inanimate that is stressed:

> Then, further, what is it that strikes the mind itself and moves it and compels it to utter wavering judgements, so that you do not believe that what has sensation can be produced from things without sensation? Surely it is because stones and pieces of wood and earth mixed together cannot produce lively sensation. But for this reason it will be right for you to remember this point here, that I do not say that sensation is produced at once from all the things that produce what has sensation, but that it matters a great deal of what size the things are that produce what has sensation, and with what shape they are endowed, and finally what they are in their movements, arrangements and positions.
>
> (Lucretius, 2.886ff.)

True, the shape and size of the constituents is stressed as well, so an allusion to the fourth, unnamed element is not *excluded* even if it is not explicit. It is one thing to claim that inanimate atoms can make up animate compounds, another to claim that certain specific inanimate substances are not enough and another is needed. However, in the immediate sequel to the very passage in book 3 in which the unnamed fourth nature is introduced, Lucretius argues that the soul-ingredients – the atoms like those which make up heat, wind and air – are mixed together in the soul in such a way that the individual natures of these compounds are not apparent in the soul, which forms, as it were, a new and distinctive whole (3.262ff.). If atoms of these types can go to make up a whole with distinct properties of its own, why should an extra type of atom be needed to explain consciousness specifically?

The problem is made even more acute in one particular context, that of free human choice. Epicurus postulated that atoms could swerve ever so slightly from a straight path, for two reasons: first so that the process of collision and rebounding could begin (Chapter Three), and second to break the inexorable sequence of cause and effect which would otherwise exist (Lucretius, 2.216–93 = LS 11H, 20F). Both Epicurus himself (*On Nature* 34.7.11 = LS 20C) and Diogenes of Oenoanda (fr. 54.III.4 Smith = LS 20G) reproach Democritus, the latter by name, on the grounds that his atomic theory, in the absence of such a swerve, removes human freedom; though whether Democritus himself drew that conclusion is uncertain. Determinism, Epicurus argues, is self-refuting; the determinist is compelled by his own position to accept that both his own belief in determinism, and his opponent's denial of it, are predetermined (*On Nature* 34.7.9 = LS 20C). It is unclear whether swerves have any significance when they happen in the world at large, outside souls, as by the principle of equilibrium they must surely do; certainly they are not needed to explain chance events in the sense of coincidences, which are quite compatible with determinism, even if not with a *providential* determinism like that of the Stoics.

The difficulty is that, while random swerves of atoms in our minds may remove inexorable necessity predetermining every thought and action, they seem to do so at the cost of introducing not responsible choice but arbitrary and unaccountable behaviour. We need not suppose that the swerve, either in human minds or outside it, introduces such a degree of randomness that all regularity and predictability is done away with; we have seen that the whole atomist tradition placed considerable emphasis on the regularity of nature within a world-system, and the claim that human behaviour is not entirely predictable need not imply that it is totally unpredictable. But still, in so far as our choices are not predetermined, but the result of random atomic swerves, it is difficult to see how they can be regarded as responsible or as something for which we are accountable; and that is so whether we suppose, with most interpreters, that the swerve is supposed to occur at the time of free choice, or whether we suppose with Furley[7] that it occurs at some unspecified point, the claim being that a continuous sequence of entirely predetermined causes cannot be traced back throughout our lives. Furley's view is based partly on comparison with other ancient discussions of responsibility, partly on the fact that Lucretius' account in 4.877ff. = LS 14E of decisions (like that to walk) makes no reference to the swerve, and partly on admitted oddities in Lucretius' account of the swerve, especially the fact that he takes as examples two cases – the race-horse starting to run when the starting-gate opens, and the person who is pushed and resists – where some delay in *reaction* is involved, as it would not be in the case of an inanimate object, but there is not much doubt what the reaction will be. This last point has led some[8] to argue that the swerve was not concerned with *free* choice at all, only with distinguishing the voluntary behaviour of living creatures from the movements of inanimate objects. But the ancient evidence concerning the swerve, in Cicero as well as in Diogenes of Oenoanda, is against this.

The answer must surely be that what is random on the level of individual atoms somehow becomes responsible on that of the whole human being or of his or her mind. This view was attributed to Epicurus in the 1920s by Bailey, but he saw it as incompatible with Epicurus' basic principles. More recently Sedley has argued that it may be only a particular application of Epicurus' general rejection of Democritean reductionism: the colour of a visible object is as real as the shapes of the colourless atoms that go to make it up, and, similarly, responsible choice can be as real as the random swerve.[9] It matters relatively little whether our choices *exploit* swerves that are among the many that are constantly occurring anyway, or whether our choices *cause* swerves of the atoms in our minds, as Sedley argues (though this is both doubtfully coherent – if all swerves are uncaused on the atomic level, it is difficult to see what it can mean to say that some are caused by choice and others not – and difficult to reconcile with the ancient evidence), or whether the swerve on the atomic level and the choice on that of the soul as a whole are simply correlated in some way.[10] The important point is that Epicurus recognises the swerve as a necessary condition for free choice, even if it is not a sufficient condition and even if the exact relation between choice and swerve remains mysterious. (Whether Epicurus was himself aware of any difficulty here we do not know.)

If, however, anti-reductionism, that the whole is greater than the sum of the parts, is rightly invoked in order to distinguish responsible choice from random swerve, this seems to make even more incongruous the postulation of the atoms of the fourth, unnamed type as necessary to explain consciousness on the grounds that atoms of heat-, wind- and air-types could not do so on their own. Once again, there is no absolute inconsistency here;[11] it might be that, while atoms of all kinds swerve (for there is no reason why the swerve should be restricted to one particular type of atom), it is only when a swerve occurs in the atoms of the fourth nature within a human soul that it takes on the special nature of free and conscious choice. There does, however, seem to be a relation here between different types of explanation that has not been fully worked out.

WHAT ARE WE?

THE STOICS

For the Stoics the human soul is that part of the all-penetrating divine spirit or *pneuma* which is present in each of us. We are thus parts of a greater whole, or, putting it the other way, our soul is the divinity within us (a theme particularly developed by the Roman Stoics, as we shall see in Chapter Seven).

Where the Epicureans explain the functioning of soul in terms of the movement and arrangement of atoms, the Stoics employ rather the notion of degrees of tension of soul-*pneuma*. For Chrysippus the souls of just people, having a greater tension, survive longer after their death (Eusebius, *Preparation for the Gospel* 15.20.6 = LS 53W; Heraclitus had said that better deaths 'share in better portions', perhaps because souls that died better deaths were more fiery: KRS pp. 207–8); they take the form of spheres (*SVF* 2.815–16) which are fiery and float upwards (Sextus, *M* 9.71) to join the heavenly fire or *aithêr*. But no individual soul can survive beyond the periodic conflagration when, as we saw in Chapter Three, the whole world is absorbed in Zeus. (Cleanthes, however, held that all souls last till the conflagration; DL 7.157).

The human soul was divided by Chrysippus into eight faculties (Calcidius, *On Plato's* Timaeus 220, cf. LS vol. 2, p. 313; 'Aëtius' 4.21.1–4 = LS 53H): the five senses, the power of reproduction, the power of speech (reflecting the Stoic emphasis on reason/speech, *logos*) and the *hêgemonikon* or 'ruling part' which most Stoics, like the Epicureans, located in the chest rather than the head, Chrysippus using the argument that emotion is felt there (Galen, *PHP* 2.7.8), that speech comes from there (ibid. 2.5.16, cf. 2.5.8ff. = LS 53U), and that, when you point to yourself saying 'this is me', you point to the upper part of your torso, not to your head, and when you say 'I' (in Greek, *egô*) you point towards your chest with your chin (ibid. 2.2.10–12 = LS 34J; Galen goes on to object that people also touch their noses when saying 'give me this', which for us may serve rather as a reminder that gestures vary from culture to culture). The other soul-faculties extend through the body from the ruling part, and are likened by 'Aëtius' (loc. cit.) to the tentacles of an octopus. The idea of *pneuma* as the instrument of soul's interaction with body had become increasingly prominent (influenced by developments in medical theory) in Aristotle's later writings and in those of his followers; the Stoics are influenced by the same developments but

67

identify soul with *pneuma* rather than regarding the latter as the instrument of the former.

The absence in the Stoic account of any faculty of the soul corresponding to the Platonic or Aristotelian desire or appetite is significant. For Chrysippus all functioning of the human ruling principle is rational – not of course in the sense that it is in accordance with right reason, but in the sense that it involves an exercise of judgement. (Something at least of the force of 'rational' in this use can perhaps be captured by 'with content capable of being expressed in propositions'; the Greek word in question, *logikos*, can after all be translated by 'verbal' as well as by 'rational'.) Assent to an impression about something and impulse towards it or away from it are thus but two sides of a single coin, as it were.

Emotions, in particular, are judgements; if we fear or desire something, that is because we received an impression that it was bad or good, and chose to assent to that impression. Since, as we shall see in Chapter Five, wickedness alone is bad and virtue alone good, to judge that anything else is bad is a misjudgement – but still a judgement; and wrong judgements turn into passions when they gather an impetus of their own, or, as Chrysippus puts it, it is rather as when, having started running, one finds it difficult to stop (Galen, *PHP* 4.2.15–18 = LS 65J). Moreover, in a passion a double judgement is involved: distress is the belief that evil is present *and* the belief that it is right to be distressed by it (pseudo-Andronicus, *On Passions* 1 = LS 65B), which explains why distress lessens over time, the first belief persisting but the second not (Galen, *PHP* 4.7.12ff. = LS 65O). Both pseudo-Andronicus and Galen speak of distress in terms of a physical contraction of the soul, and that is characteristic; the mental and the physical are not separate for the Stoics.

Even a Stoic sage is going to feel an initial chill at an apparent threat; but fear takes over when one mistakenly accepts that the threat really does involve harm to oneself (mistakenly, because being wicked oneself is the only evil, and it is entirely in one's own power). The initial reaction is not voluntary, and not morally significant; the important thing is not to be carried along by it and believe that real evil threatens or real harm has been done. This at least is what is suggested by two passages from later, Roman Stoics, which probably reflect early Stoic doctrine too:

WHAT ARE WE?

And so that you may know how passions begin, grow and are carried away, there is a first impulse (*motus*) which is not voluntary, a sort of preparation for passion and a sort of threatening. The second is with a wish which is not stubborn, such as: it is right for me to avenge myself, since I have been harmed, or for this person to be punished, because he has done wrong. The third is an impulse which is now out of control, which wants to be avenged not [just] if it is right, but in any case, and has conquered reason. We cannot by reason escape that first blow on the mind, just as we cannot escape those things which we said happen to our bodies, so that somebody else's yawning will not encourage us [to yawn], our eyes not blink when fingers are suddenly pointed towards them. Reason cannot overcome these [reactions], but habit and constant practice may perhaps weaken them. The second impulse, which derives from a judgement, is removed by a judgement.

(Seneca, *On Anger* 2.4.1)

Things seen by the mind, which the philosophers call impressions, by which the human mind is immediately struck at the first appearance of a thing that affects it, are not subject to will or judgement, but introduce themselves into people by a certain force of their own so that they notice them. But the approvals, which they call assents, by which the same things seen [by the mind] are recognised, are voluntary and come about by people's judgement. For this reason, when some frightening sound occurs from the sky or the collapse [of a building], or there is sudden news of some danger, or anything else of this sort happens, the wise person's mind too is necessarily moved for a moment and shrinks and grows pale, not because it has formed an opinion of some evil, but through certain swift and unconsidered changes that forestall the functioning of mind and reason .... But the wise person, after his colour and expression have changed briefly and superficially, does not assent, but retains the stability and strength of the opinion which he has always had about appearances of this sort, as being not at all to be feared but rather terrifying us with a false appearance and empty fear.

(Epictetus, fr. 9: part = LS 65Y)

The idea that some bite or sting will remain even if grief proper is not felt appears already in Cicero, *Tusculan Disputations* 3.83, and a similar idea is attributed to Zeno by Seneca, *On Anger* 3.16.7 (cf. LS vol. 2, p. 417).

Passions – pleasure, distress, desire and fear, and their many subdivisions (DL 7.110) – are all bad because they reflect wrong judgements about supposed present and future good and evil;[12] but in saying that the sage is without passions, *apathês*, the Stoics did not intend to banish all feelings, since the sage will have 'good feelings' (*eupatheiai*). Corresponding to desire and fear there are 'wish' and 'caution' or 'wise avoidance', and corresponding to pleasure there is 'joy' (DL 7.116 = LS 65F). 'Joy' and 'wish' relate to the one true good, virtue, present and continuing in the future respectively; 'caution' will be the avoidance of wrong-doing. There is no 'good feeling' corresponding to pain, i.e. relating to present evil, for this would be grief at one's own real evil, i.e. wickedness; for the sage this is obviously irrelevant, and even for the non-virtuous person the correct reaction is not to be distressed at one's own shortcomings but to attempt improvement.[13] The Stoic approach to virtue is an all-or-nothing one, as we shall see in Chapter Five, and since grief at one's own wickedness is irrelevant to the sage, it cannot be a good feeling.[14]

Since all passions are judgements, and there is no separate part of the soul concerned with desire, it would seem that there cannot for Chrysippus, strictly speaking, be a conflict between reason and desire in the individual soul. And we are told that he regarded apparent conflicts as in fact rapid waverings of our judgement, approving first one course of action and then another, the wavering or oscillation of judgement being so rapid that we are unaware of it (Plutarch, *On Moral Virtue* 446F = LS 65G). The changeability of these judgements is directly attributed to their 'weakness', on which see Chapter Two. This theory has been criticised by Brad Inwood[15] for postulating an explanation which is not only in principle unobservable but actually at variance with our direct experience; but it may still be thought to give a more plausible account of what happens where we struggle to control our desires than does the Platonic picture (Plato, *Republic* 4 439) of separate parts of the soul in conflict with each other, which raises problems about just what constitutes the real 'us'. The oscillation theory may, however, owe some of its plausibility to the demands of dramatic presentation. We know from Galen, *PHP* 4.6.19, that

Chrysippus used as an example the myth of Medea, who killed her children when her better judgement was overcome by desire for revenge, and the tragedian Euripides, in giving the classic portrayal of the same story, made use of a soliloquy in which Medea expresses first one side of the conflict and then the other. It is difficult to see how else the experience could be *communicated* or represented; but it may not follow from this that wavering between alternatives is an accurate analysis of the experience itself.

A later Stoic, Posidonius, returned to a position more like Plato's, through dissatisfaction with Chrysippus' account in its relation to the observed facts of human psychological development from childhood to adulthood. For Posidonius, as for Plato, moral improvement must include a training of the irrational part of the soul, starting in childhood. The logical implication of Chrysippus' position on the other hand, like Socrates', is that the way to make people good is by reasoning with them. Historically it was the Platonic doctrine of the divided soul that prevailed – one may suspect, because of the double attraction (especially for preachers) of being able to exhort people to side with the better 'part of themselves', on the one hand, and of being able to console wrong-doers by saying that it was not the best part of them that wanted to do wrong, on the other.

Moreover, it is not clear that Chrysippus' position was quite so clear-cut as the foregoing account would suggest. It is difficult, in spite of LS p. 422, to interpret the comparison of passion to the person who wants to stop running, but cannot, simply in terms of an impulse not in accordance with *right* reason.[16] For the image suggests a contrast between two *separate* forces, the will which wants to stop and the body which cannot. Posidonius, at least, saw Chrysippus' own image as having dualistic implications,[17] and it certainly suggests a rather different picture from the oscillation between different judgements described by Plutarch. Admittedly, Plutarch distinguishes the way in which our judgement is supposed to oscillate from the way in which we ourselves experience the apparent conflict, and the image of the person who cannot stop running may be an analogy for the latter rather than the former.

We need not in any case suppose that Posidonius would have regarded his disagreement with Chrysippus as challenging the entire Stoic school; there is a danger in identifying Stoic views too narrowly with those of Chrysippus in particular, and Posidonius may have felt that he was giving a better interpretation of the original Stoic position than Chrysippus had done. Certainly we are told by Galen that Zeno did not *identify* passions and judgements, as Chrysippus did:

> Chrysippus then in the first book [of] *On the Passions* endeavours to show that the passions are certain judgements of the reasoning part of the soul, while Zeno thinks that the passions are not the judgements themselves, but the contractions and relaxations, exaltations and depressions of the soul that supervene on these.
>
> (Galen, *PHP* 5.1.4)

And Galen cites Posidonius as appealing to Cleanthes for a conflict between reason and desire (*PHP* 5.6.34 = LS 65I), though first Posidonius' and then Galen's interpretations of statements by earlier philosophers need to be treated with caution; we have already seen that Chrysippus himself could make statements that could be interpreted in a similar way, and Galen at least is a tendentious witness, being concerned to contrast Chrysippus' views with Platonic doctrine to the advantage of the latter and the detriment of the former.

Another way in which the stress on reason and cognition in early Stoic psychology may have been modified is by an increased emphasis on the notion of will in the Roman Stoics in particular. It is something of a commonplace to contrast ancient Greek intellectualism in ethics with Latin voluntarism; as with many commonplaces it contains some truth, the question is how much. Greek intellectualism is associated above all with Socrates, for whom all wrongdoing was simply ignorance (a view which the Stoics shared), but it can be traced in a more attenuated form in many aspects of ancient Greek thought.[18] And it is striking that the presentation of what we know as the free-will debate in terms of freedom of the *will* occurs first in Cicero and Lucretius; Greek sources speak rather of whether we are free or whether anything is up to us. The outburst of Juvenal's termagant,

> This is what I want, this is what I'm telling you to do, my
> wanting it all the reason you're going to get
> (*hoc volo, sic iubeo, sit pro ratione voluntas*)
>
> (Juvenal, *Satires* 6.223)

is difficult to imagine in classical Greek form; the very word for 'to will' in Greek, *boulesthai*, though etymologically cognate with

Latin *voluntas* and English 'will', has overtones of counsel, deliber-
ation, judgement.

The character Meno, in Plato's dialogue of that name, had suggested a definition of virtue as 'to desire fine things and be able
to get them' (77B). Socrates then argued that everyone desires fine
things, though they may be mistaken about which things are in
fact fine, and that it is therefore only the second part of Meno's
definition, the ability, that really counts (78B). Pretty clearly, an
important part of 'being able' will constitute *knowing* which things
to aim for. Seneca and Epictetus make the same point, though in
terms of wishing or wanting rather than desiring: the important
thing is the knowledge rather than the wish (Seneca, *Letters on
Morals* 81.13; Epictetus, *Discourses* 2.14.10). But elsewhere we find
Seneca making *wanting* crucial:

> [Athletes] need much food and drink, much oil, and finally
> long effort; you will get virtue without equipment or expense.
> Whatever can make you good is in your possession. What
> do you need in order to be good? To want to be (*velle*).
>
> (Seneca, *Letters on Morals* 80.3–4)

True, there need be no actual inconsistency here, for Seneca may
be presupposing that wanting to be good depends on knowing
what real goodness is; the context is concerned with exercising the
mind and with setting oneself free from unreal fears. But it is not
in terms of knowledge or ignorance that the point is actually put in
the immediate context. Seneca is engaging in rhetorical exhortation
rather than philosophical analysis; but the emphasis on will nevertheless seems significant.[19]

Seneca also in one passage has impulse preceding assent:

> Every rational creature does nothing unless it is first aroused
> by the impression of some thing, *then* gets an impulse and
> *then assent confirms this impulse.* Let me say what assent is.
> I ought to walk; I finally walk just at the time when I have
> said this to myself and approved this opinion of mine.
>
> (Seneca, *Letters on Morals* 113.18: my emphasis)

This seems un-Chrysippean (and is to be distinguished from the
initial involuntary reaction to imagined threat or injury discussed
earlier).[20] For Chrysippus the impulse is produced by the assent, or
perhaps better *is* the assent under a different description. However,
impulse preceding assent does appear in another source reflecting

early Stoic discussions, and it has been suggested that it may there be an allusion to views held by Zeno.[21] Once again, it may be misleading to regard early Stoic views as uniform, and later views as a deviation from a uniform earlier orthodoxy.

For the Stoics all our actions are as much parts of the universal causal nexus which is fate, providence or God, and so as much predetermined, as any other events. Critics argued that if this were so we could neither be praised for our good deeds nor blamed for bad ones. But Chrysippus argued for the compatibility of determinism on the one hand and responsibility, praise and blame on the other, doing so on two main grounds. First, even if our reactions to external influences, to situations and the impressions they produce in us, are predetermined, they are still *our* reactions; just as, if you push a cylinder and a cone they will roll in different ways, the fact both that they roll at all and that they roll in different ways reflects their own shapes rather than the fact that you pushed them:

> 'Although it is the case', Chrysippus said, 'that all things are constrained and bound together by fate through a certain necessary and primary principle, yet the way in which the natures of our minds themselves are subject to fate depends on their own individual quality. For if they have been fashioned through nature originally in a healthy and expedient way, they pass on all that force, which assails them from outside through fate, in a more placid and pliant manner. If, however, they are harsh and ignorant and uncultured, and not sustained by any supports from good practices, then even if they are pressed on by little or no necessity from an adverse fate, through their own perversity and voluntary impulse they hurl themselves into constant crimes and errors. And that this very thing should come about in this way is a result of that natural and necessary sequence which is called fate. For it is, as it were, fated and a consequence of their type itself, that bad natures should not lack crimes and errors.
>
> Then he employs an illustration of approximately this point which is certainly not lacking in relevance or wit. 'It is', he says, 'just as if you throw a cylindrical stone across a region of ground which is sloping and steep; you were the cause and beginning of headlong fall for it, but soon it rolls

headlong, not because *you* are now bringing that about, but because that is how its fashion and the capacity for rolling in its shape are. Just so the rule and principle and necessity of fate sets kinds and beginnings of causes in motion, but the impulses of our minds and deliberations, and our actions themselves, are governed by each person's own will and by the natures of our minds.'

(Gellius, *Attic Nights* 7.2.7–11 = LS 62D)[22]

It is not, of course, to be supposed from this that Chrysippus regards human reactions to situations as no more complex than the 'reaction' of a cylindrical object to being pushed; the point is rather that, even if human reactions are predetermined in a much more complex way than those of inanimate objects, they are predetermined – but are still ours. The fact that the developed character, which causes us to react as we do, is itself the product of earlier influences, and ultimately of those which existed even before our birth, is not felt to be an objection to this; and the fact that people behave in the way their natures lead them to can be a consolation to those on the receiving end of their actions:

These things are naturally done by people of that sort, of necessity. The person who wants this not to be so wants the fig to be without its sour juice. In general remember this, that within a very short time both you and he will be dead; and after a short while not even your names will survive.

(Marcus Aurelius, *Meditations* 4.6)

Second, responsibility is maintained in a determinist system because our actions make a difference even though they are predetermined; to say that certain things are fated to happen does not mean that they are fated to happen regardless of what anyone does beforehand, but rather that certain outcomes and the actions which are necessary to bring them about are 'co-fated' with one another. It would be absurd to say that Laius, the father of the mythological Oedipus, would have a child whether he slept with a woman or not[23] – the point presumably being that, once Laius had been warned by the oracle that if he had a child that child would kill him, it was his taking the risk of sleeping with Jocasta his wife that brought about the fated outcome, and that was *his* responsibility (even though predetermined). For the Stoics God, or fate, sets tasks for mortals in which they will choose rightly or wrongly.[24] Ancient critics of Stoicism found it scandalous that the gods should do this knowing that the mortals would fail, but the Stoic reply would be that it was the mortals' own responsibility that they failed. Moreover, in the story the oracle to Laius was itself a punishment for Laius' earlier crime in seducing the son of Pelops – coincidentally named Chrysippus; though we do not know whether the historical Chrysippus discussed this point.

Although for the Stoics all people are responsible for their actions, only the sage is free (DL 7.121 = LS 67M). For freedom consists in never having one's desires thwarted, and the sage accepts whatever happens as providentially ordained for the best:

> And here we suppose that the task of the philosopher is to make his wish[es] fit what happens, so that neither does any of the things that happen do so against our will nor does any of the things that do not happen fail to happen with us wanting it to. From this it comes about for those who achieve this that they neither fail in their desire nor encounter what they are trying to avoid, and that they spend their lives without distress, fear or anxiety.
>
> (Epictetus, *Discourses* 2.14.7–8)

That is not to say that the sage can anticipate everything that will happen; only the gods can do that. Nor yet is it to say that Stoicism is a philosophy of inaction, though it can be misunderstood as such, just as Epicureanism can be misunderstood as a philosophy of self-indulgence (see Chapter Five). Rather, just because even the sage does not know everything that the future holds in store, he will act in whatever way seems appropriate given the degree of understanding of the future he does have and his knowledge of general principles; but he will always act 'with reservation', being prepared to accept, if things go against his original intention, that it is better that they should do so:

> The wise person does not change his plan when all those things are still present which were present when he adopted it. For this reason it never occurs to him to repent, because nothing could have been done better at the time than what was done, nor any better decision have been reached than what was decided. But he approaches everything with the

reservation 'if nothing occurs to impede it'. And for this reason we say that he is successful in everything and that nothing happens contrary to his expectation, because he has already taken it into account in his mind that something could intervene to prevent what he has decided upon.

(Seneca, *On Good Deeds* 4.34.4-5; cf. Stobaeus, *Selections* 2.7.11s, p. 115.5 Wachsmuth–Hense = LS 65W)

To say that it is 'better' that one's original intention be thwarted may indeed mean 'better for the universe as a whole' (see Chapter Three, on divine providence). But the individual's true interest is that of the whole of which he or she is one small part. Moreover, as Epictetus in particular emphasises (cf. e.g. *Discourses* 1.1.7–9 = LS 62K), the important thing is to be able to distinguish between what is in our power – our attitude to events and our own initiatives, which as being virtuous or wicked are the only things that matter – and what is not in our control, namely external events and the success or failure of our undertakings.

The freedom of the sage was illustrated by the image of a dog tied to a wagon; it can follow voluntarily or be dragged, but it will follow none the less:

And [Zeno and Chrysippus] themselves emphasised that everything was according to fate using the following example, that if a dog is tied, as it were, to a wagon, then if the dog wishes to follow, it will both be pulled and follow, acting by its own choice together with the necessity; but if it does not wish to follow, it will in any case be compelled. The same I suppose applies to human beings; even if they do not wish to follow they will in any case be compelled to go where fate decrees.

(Hippolytus, *Philos.* 21 = LS 62A)

Similarly Cleanthes' prayer, cited by Epictetus, *Manual* 53 = LS 62B: 'Lead me, Zeus, and you too, Fate, to the place for which I am appointed by you; for I shall follow without hesitating. But if I am unwilling, becoming wicked, I shall follow none the less.' Seneca, *Letters on Morals* 107.11, translates this into Latin verse and adds at the end the line: 'The Fates lead the person who is willing, but drag the one who is unwilling.' To make the image complete we should perhaps suppose that the wagon – standing for fate, or the course of events – occasionally changes its direction in ways that even the most compliant dog cannot anticipate; the wise dog, as it were, will at once change course to follow the wagon.

But, it may be objected, if everything is predetermined it will be predetermined that some dogs follow in a docile fashion and others struggle in vain resistance. Yes indeed; but because following in a docile fashion or resisting is one's *own* action, it is, on Stoic principles, one's own responsibility. And that is just as well, for if we try to introduce any greater, non-Stoic degree of freedom of action into the picture we risk making it absurd. If, for example, we suppose that our actions are predetermined but our attitudes 'free' in some sense that excludes determinism, we will attribute to the Stoics the absurdity that if a person is predestined to be a burglar, say, his burgling is beyond his control but his attitude to it is not – so that the important thing is not whether he is a burglar but that he should feel bad about being one. That clearly cannot be the Stoic view (even if they had recognised kleptomania, they would hardly have made it the basis of their whole moral theory). Rather, our attitudes, the actions we attempt, their outcomes, successful or otherwise, and things that happen to us are *all* predetermined; the difference is that the first two are in our power in Stoic terms (and naturally linked to each other, as they must be in any plausible psychological theory), while the last two are ultimately beyond our power to influence.

There are indeed people who do wrong but feel they shouldn't; but for them the Stoic answer is not 'since you're doing wrong, it must be fated that you do, so accept it' but rather 'try and follow your better instincts'. If they do wrong, that is predetermined, but if they reform, that is too; the crucial point is that, for the Stoics, determinism does not remove responsibility either for doing wrong or for reforming yourself.

CARNEADES

Questions of determinism, responsibility and freedom have bulked large in this chapter; and that is no accident, for these issues are closely connected with our sense of our own identity and our place in the universe. It was also on these topics that the Academic sceptic Carneades made two striking contributions, criticising both Epicurean and Stoic views and anticipating modern discussions;

though his intervention was arguably more successful in one case than in the other.

Aristotle had raised (in *On Interpretation* 9) the problem of the truth or falsity of statements made before the event about things that might either happen or not. If the prior statement that the event would occur was true, it would seem that it could not but occur; and similarly that it could not occur if the statement was false. Aristotle's own reaction to the paradox is unclear, but both the Epicureans and the Stoics regarded the problem as a real one. Their responses were, however, diametrically opposed to each other. Epicurus and his followers held that some future events are not predetermined, because of the atomic swerve, and accordingly that some future-tense statements are neither true nor false – much to Cicero's annoyance; Cicero objects in particular to the implication that the disjunction 'Either Philoctetes will be wounded or he will not be' could have been true, though neither 'Philoctetes will be wounded' nor 'Philoctetes will not be wounded' was true (Cicero, *On Fate* 37 = LS 20H).

The Stoics on the other hand, holding that all events *are* predetermined, supported this view not indeed by arguing that the truth of a future-tense statement itself caused the event necessarily to occur (which would be a confusion of the physical and the logical), but by pointing to the problem that would exist concerning the truth of future-tense statements if all events were not predetermined.

Against both Epicureans and Stoics Carneades argued, anticipating Gilbert Ryle,[25] that the truth or falsity of future-tense statements has no implications in itself for whether the events referred to are predetermined or not (Cicero, *On Fate* 19–20 and 27–8 = LS 70G). To say that a prediction of what will happen is true is simply to explain the meaning of the word 'true' (in a way that identifies the truth of a statement with its correspondence to the facts, the standard approach to truth in ancient Greek philosophy).[26] Or, as we might put it, 'what will be will be' is a truism, but just for that reason it says nothing about the predetermined necessity or otherwise of the events referred to.

On this question Carneades was assuredly right. More controversial is his other contribution to the debate, on the question of the causes of free human action. The Stoics had argued that to deny universal determinism would be to introduce 'uncaused movements' – like the Epicurean atomic swerve – and so to disrupt the unity of the universe as a causal system. (See Chapter Three.) Against this Carneades argued that human freedom could be maintained without the need for the atomic swerve, and indeed that Epicurus would have been better off without it; free human choices are not predetermined, but yet are not uncaused, for the cause is in the nature of the voluntary action itself (Cicero, *On Fate* 23ff. = LS 20E). This position anticipates modern theories of 'agent causation' like that advanced by Richard Taylor;[27] but to some at least, including the present writer, it seems unsatisfactory as a solution.[28] Claiming that the cause of the action lies in the agent, or that human choices are different in kind from physical events and must be discussed in different terms, does not alter the fact that *on* the level of physical events – which human choices surely affect – either every outcome is the inevitable consequence of the preceding situation, or else it is not. There is no way out of this dilemma, at any rate if we suppose that the discussion relates to a closed system, successive states of which can at least in principle be described. The Stoic system is definitely of this type; and while the Epicurean universe is spatially infinite, the fact that the speed of the atoms is finite, though very great, means that it is only the position and movement of a finite number of atoms that have to be taken into account in considering the antecedents, a finite time beforehand, of any particular event. Epicurus was right to see the atomic swerve, or some corresponding non-deterministic event, as at least a necessary condition for freedom from determinism, even if not a full explanation of it, and Carneades was wrong to suggest that the swerve could have been dispensed with.

A further problem relates to Carneades' own position. As a sceptic, was he simply pointing out that, even if neither the Epicurean nor the Stoic position was convincing, they did not exhaust the possibilities, and claiming that there was a third theoretical possibility both concerning the truth of future-tense statements and concerning the causes of human actions? Or was he himself maintaining that there actually *are* events, especially but not only human actions,[29] that are not predetermined but yet have causes? And, if he *was* maintaining the latter, what was he, as a sceptic, doing in making such an assertion? Long at one time explained this by suggesting[30] that the claim of human freedom was an exception in that it is a matter of our immediate personal experience in the same way that our sensations are, as opposed to claims about the external world. But the suggestion is dropped in LS (p. 465), and that Carneades did intend a positive claim about human freedom is at best uncertain. His own claim need only be that free will is *possible* without a swerve, not that it actually exists, and that the truth of future-tense statements does not in itself imply that the events referred to are predetermined, whether or not they are so in fact.

5

HOW CAN I BE HAPPY?

THE CENTRAL QUESTION OF ETHICS

The opposition between Epicureanism and Stoicism is as marked in their ethics as anywhere; and disagreements over how best to live one's life are going to have more practical consequences, and be more noted by society at large, than disagreements over such issues as the infinite divisibility of matter. But once again there are also similarities between the two schools, and indeed with the sceptical schools as well. These similarities are of two types, first those concerning the basic framework of the discussion, and second those concerning some, though only some, of the practical attitudes that the schools recommend.

For the Epicureans and the Stoics, as for other ancient Greek thinkers and notably for Aristotle, the basic question of ethics is not 'what sort of actions are right?' but 'what sort of person should I be?', or 'what life-style and policies should I adopt?' The very term 'ethics' is derived from êthos, which means 'character'. The sort of person one is and the life-style one adopts will indeed have an immediate bearing on the actions one performs, and both Stoics and Epicureans would agree with Aristotle (*EN* 1.8) that character cannot be divorced from action – you cannot be a just or courageous person if you behave in an unjust or cowardly fashion; but the emphasis of an ethics that centres upon characters and life-styles is going to be different from that of one that centres upon actions. And that is why I have formulated the title of this chapter in a way that includes a reference to the agent.

This, however, carries with it a further implication. If the primary concern of ethics is with how it is best for me to live, then even when it has been established what sort of actions are 'right', there remains the question whether performing such actions is the best way for me to live, and if so why. (Unless, indeed, we simply *define* 'right actions' as the ones it is best for me to perform.) Even Plato in the *Republic* has Socrates commend justice to others by the rewards it brings to oneself, not indeed the material rewards (though once the argument is concluded these are rather optimistically added in; 612D–614A) or rewards in the next world (614A ff.), but the intrinsic reward of happiness which justice brings (361C; 367D; 445A; 588A ff.).

The difference between the ancient Greek ethics of personal 'happiness' and the Kantian ideals of duty which prevailed until quite recently (at least in what people *said*) can be captured by the thought that for the former 'why should I do what is right?' is a question requiring an answer, while for the latter it no more admits or requires an answer than does 'why should I believe what is true?' In 1960 Arthur Adkins could, famously, declare that 'We are all Kantians now';[1] but already in 1974 Sir Kenneth Dover could comment on this that 'Unless I am seriously deceiving myself, I and most of the people I know well find the Greeks of the Classical period easier to understand than Kantians.'[2] Nevertheless, in the mid-1970s first-year Classics undergraduates were in my experience still shocked, ostensibly anyway, at the suggestion that one might need a reason for doing what one accepted was right. Not so more recently – which may just show that moral discourse has become more realistic than it used to be. Perhaps, then, reflecting on ancient Greek moral discourse may have something to tell us about the terms in which discussions *might* (not 'should') be framed, even if we do not accept the ancients' conclusions.

For Aristotle it was axiomatic that all people both naturally pursue, and ought to pursue, *eudaimonia* – conventionally, and subsequently in this book, translated into English by 'happiness', sometimes translated instead by 'flourishing', but essentially the sort of life that brings satisfaction and of which we congratulate or 'felicitate' the possessors. And this approach was shared by Aristotle's successors. Being 'happy' and being a 'good' person necessarily go together; but 'a good person' means not so much a morally virtuous one (though moral virtue is a necessary and important component of goodness and happiness for Aristotle, a necessary component of it for Epicurus, and identical with it for the Stoics) as a human being who is living the best life for a human being. The question, for Plato, Aristotle, Epicureans and Stoics alike, is what sort of life is best, what sort of life constitutes 'happiness'.

It follows that ethics for both Epicureans and Stoics is self-referential; the agent is concerned with how he or she can achieve a happy life, with what is the good for *me*. Here, however, there is a danger of misunderstanding. There are aspects of both Stoic and Epicurean ethics that may seem to a modern sensibility selfish and self-regarding in a bad sense, inconsiderate of others and lacking in humanity. But these features need not be the inevitable consequence of adopting a self-referential approach to ethics. In much modern thought, influenced by Christianity, there is a polar opposition between altruism on the one hand and selfishness on the other; if we think of ourselves *at all*, this view would imply, we must be sacrificing the interests of others to our own in a selfish and reprehensible fashion.

Aristotle is aware, to be sure, that there can be such a thing as bad self-love. But he does not regard it as the only kind. And in this he is surely right; concern that one should oneself be the best sort of person possible and live the happiest life may well involve actions for the benefit of others, if these are characteristic of the good and happy person. There may be a more realistic hope of encouraging people to act in the interests of others, if doing so is seen as being a part of acting in one's own true interest too, rather than self-interest and acting in the interest of others being necessarily antithetical. Such at least seems to be the ancient perspective, and we will have cause to return to it not only in this chapter but also in the next.

THE EPICUREANS

For Epicurus the goal of life is pleasure, and the happy life is that with most pleasure and least pain. But this does not mean, as might be thought, the life of perpetual physical self-indulgence – though Epicurus already in his own lifetime protested against those who understood him so (*ad Men.* 131 = LS 21B5), and Sedley has shown[3] that a former follower of Epicurus, Timocrates, who quarrelled with him, was partly responsible for encouraging such misunderstandings. Misunderstandings were probably, however, inevitable.

For Epicurus, the limit of pleasure is the removal of pain – both physical pain and mental anxiety. Once pain has been removed, anything further can only be a 'variation' (*poikilmos*) – a 'seasoning', as it were – of pleasure; it cannot increase it, and so it can be dispensed with:

> The limit of magnitude of pleasures is the removal of all pain. Wherever pleasure is present, for as long as it is present, there is neither pain, nor distress, nor the combination of the two.
>
> (*PD* 3 = LS 21C)

> Pleasure is not increased, but only varied in the flesh, when once what caused pain because of lack has been removed.
>
> (*PD* 18 = LS 21E)

Lavish banquets may give variety to life, but they do not bring a greater degree of pleasure than does simple food, provided that such food is enough to dispel hunger:

> We think that self-sufficiency is a great good, not in order to use only a little in every case, but so that we can make use of a little when we do not have much; being genuinely persuaded that the people who have the most pleasant enjoyment of extravagance are those who need it least, and that everything which is natural is easily obtained, while it is what is empty that is hard to obtain. Simple flavours give as much pleasure as an extravagant diet, whenever all the pain due to lack is removed; and barley-bread and water produce the summit of pleasure, whenever someone in need consumes them.
>
> (*ad Men.* 130–1 = LS 21B)

[How blind you are] not to see that nature barks for nothing else for itself, except that pain should be absent and removed from the body, and that in the mind it should enjoy pleasant sensation with anxiety and fear banished? So we see that for our bodily nature few things altogether are needed, whatever can remove pain, and also furnish many delights. Nature herself on each occasion requires nothing more welcome, even if there are not golden statues of young men throughout the house holding flaming lamps in their right hands to provide light for night-time banquets,[4] and the house does not shine with silver and glitter with gold, and gilded coffered ceilings do not echo to the lyre – when lying down together in soft grass beside a stream of water beneath the branches of a lofty tree people pleasantly relax[5] without great wealth, especially when the weather smiles on them and the season of the year sprinkles the green grass with flowers. Nor do hot fevers leave the body more swiftly if you toss under embroidered cloths and ruddy purple, than if you have to lie under the common person's cloak.

(Lucretius, 2.16–36 = LS 21W)

Or more succinctly: 'He who knows the limits of life knows that what removes pain due to want and renders the whole of life complete is easily obtained; so that there is no need of deeds which involve competition' (*PD* 21 = LS 24C).

The Epicurean will enjoy banquets and the good things of life if possible, provided of course he or she does so in moderation and in a way that will not bring more pain in the long run. Epicurus is not an advocate of asceticism like those Platonists or Christians who argued that bodily pleasures were a hindrance to intellectual or spiritual advance. But the Epicurean will not be anxious about maintaining a social and financial position which will ensure the continued availability of banquets, for such security cannot in fact be achieved for certain, and the anxieties involved in the attempt are likely to spoil the enjoyment one would otherwise have; and general frugality makes us more able to appreciate the occasional luxury properly (*ad Men.* 131 = LS 21B):

The anxiety of the soul is not removed, nor any joy worth mentioning produced, either by the presence of the greatest wealth or by honour and notability among the multitude or by anything else of what comes from causes *that know no limit.*

(Epicurus, *Vatican Sayings* 81 = LS 21H; my emphasis)

All pleasures *qua* pleasant are good, but just for that very reason (*ad Men.* 129 = LS 21B) we need to be discriminating to ensure our course of action will not bring us more pain in the long run. Desires can for Epicurus be divided into three types: the natural and necessary, the natural but non-necessary, and the unnatural and non-necessary; the necessary desires are further subdivided into some of which the satisfaction is necessary for happiness, others for the body's being free from disturbance, others for life itself (ibid. 127 = LS 21B). The necessary desires will presumably include those for food, drink, and shelter, without which we cannot live; for sex, if that is what is referred to by 'the body's being free from disturbance'; and, presumably, for happiness, desire for freedom from anxiety. Natural but non-necessary desires will include those for specific types of food and drink, which are not necessary but bring us natural pleasure if we can get them.[6] And examples of the unnatural desires will include ambition for fame and political power, which many, according to Epicurus and Lucretius, regard as the route to happiness, though in fact they are impelled by a desire for security (which results, whether they know it or not, from the fear of death, as we shall see later), and their ambition will bring them disappointment and misery rather than happiness:

> Some people wished to become famous and conspicuous, thinking that in this way they would achieve security from people. So if such people's life is secure, they have gained what is naturally good; but if it is not secure, they have not gained that which they desired in the first place because it was naturally appropriate.
>
> (PD 7 = LS 22C)

> If anyone would steer his life by true reasoning, it is great riches for a person to be able to live thriftily with equanimity; for there is never shortage of a little. But people have wanted to be famous and powerful, so that their fortune might rest on a sure foundation and so that in their wealth they could live a tranquil life – all in vain, for by striving to reach the highest honour they have made the path a hostile one, and when they reach the top envy strikes them like a thunderbolt and casts them down in time, despised, to the foul pit ... so let them wearily sweat blood to no purpose, struggling along the narrow path of ambition, since their wisdom comes from others' mouths and their search is based on what they have heard rather than on the evidence of their own senses.
>
> (Lucretius, 5.1117 ff. = LS 22L)

The best way to achieve security and happiness is rather to withdraw from public life and dwell with a circle of like-minded friends, as Epicurus did in the Garden that gave its name to his school, enjoying the good things of life when one can but being aware how little one really needs.

One might expect that some non-natural desires do bring a degree of pleasure if satisfied, but not enough to justify the anxiety and possible subsequent actual pain involved, while others may be so misguided as never to bring any pleasure at all. If Epicurus was to claim that no non-natural desire ever brings any pleasure, he would be committed to claiming that those who think they enjoy pleasure from such sources are simply deluded. On the face of it, it seems more plausible to say that they are right about the pleasure but wrong about its inevitable concomitants. In conformity with Epicurus' general theory of knowledge, pleasure and pain are sensations which show us the truth about good and evil, and cannot themselves be in error, though we may err in our *opinions* about how to achieve the greatest pleasure. Nevertheless, the description of non-natural desires as 'vain' or 'empty' (*ad Men.* 127 = LS 21B) does rather suggest that their satisfaction brings no pleasure at all. Perhaps, as we shall see below, the point is that the anxiety and frustration which Epicurus sees as accompanying a life spent in pursuit of non-natural desires will be so great that they will prevent any pleasure at all being felt; if this seems an exaggerated claim, Epicurus' and still more Lucretius' desire to persuade us to a certain way of life need to be borne in mind. Certainly all non-natural desire is misguided and should be eliminated.

The tradition of recommending satisfaction with what one has goes back at least to Democritus (KRS 594). Seneca (*Letters on Morals* 21.7–9) cites Epicurus for it and continues by saying

> These utterances shouldn't be thought to be Epicurus'; they are public property. I think one should do in philosophy what customarily happens in the Senate; when someone proposes something which pleases me in part, I tell him to divide his proposal into two parts, and I support what I approve.

The question, however, arises: just what is the basis on which Epicurus determines that some desires are natural and others non-natural? That pleasure is the good he argued, notoriously, from observation of animals as soon as they are born (Cicero, *On Ends* 1.30 = LS 21A; the so-called 'cradle argument', which we will meet again, used for a very different purpose, in a Stoic context). Is it by a similar criterion that desires are judged natural or otherwise,

which would suggest the elimination of the artificialities of civilisation and a 'back-to-nature' ethics? Or is the criterion rather that
experience shows (in Epicurus' view) that we are better off not
trying to fulfil certain desires which are *therefore* dismissed as
non-natural? Would Epicurus cope with the claims of rival life-
styles by arguing that their proponents were wrong about human
nature, perhaps all nature (rather as Plato makes Socrates in the
Gorgias argue that Callicles is wrong: 508A)? Or would he rather
try to convince us that experience shows that lives based on other
principles will not achieve happiness in practice? Perhaps, indeed,
both; Lucretius 5.1117ff., quoted on p. 87, refers to the ambitious
being guided by other people's opinions rather than their own
experience. However, while Lucretius' account of the development
of civilisation in his fifth book stresses the problems sophisti-
cation brings – a common theme of Roman literature – it does
not idealise the primitive condition. Indeed, it has been well
argued[7] that in relation to this issue book 5 should be interpreted not as self-contained but as leading up to the prologue of
book 6 which stresses the blessings Epicureanism brings. What
matters is not whether your circumstances are primitive or civil-
ised, impoverished or luxurious, but the attitude you have towards
them.

But even if we can establish to our satisfaction which desires
are natural and which not, it may still be objected that the sort of
restrained happiness which Epicurus offers is still going to be hard
for most people to achieve. Are not pains and losses of various
sorts things about which we are necessarily going to be anxious?
Here the Epicurean answer is twofold. The third *Principal Doctrine*, which asserts that the limit of pleasure is the removal of
pain, is immediately followed by the fourth, which asserts that
no pain is both great and long-lasting (LS 21C). In the conditions
of ancient medicine that was perhaps truer than now; great pain
was likely to be swiftly followed by death (or recovery), while in
chronic illness, Epicurus argued, there is actually more bodily
pleasure present than pain, if (one may add) we choose to be
aware of it. And second, physical pain can be outweighed by
mental pleasure. The body, or as Epicurus puts it 'the flesh' (see
Chapter Four) is confined to the present moment, while the mind
can range over past and future (DL 10.136 = LS 21R; Cicero,
Tusculan Disputations 5.95 = LS 21T). This suggests that
unfounded anxieties about the future cause even more distress than

does physical pain; it also implies that the memory of past happiness can outweigh present physical pain. And so Epicurus, dying after a fortnight's illness with kidney-stone (DL 10.15) which had earlier prompted him to write 'For seven days before writing this I have been unable to pass urine, and there have been pains of the type that bring people to their last day' (Epicurus, fr. 36 Bailey), wrote to his friend Idomeneus

> Passing this happy day of my life, and dying, I write this to you. The strangury and the affliction in my guts are progressing, lacking no excess in their severity; but set against all these things is the joy in my soul at the memory of the discussions we have had.
>
> (DL 10.22 = LS 24D)

The wise person will be *happy* when tortured on the rack, even though he or she will cry out and lament (DL 10.118 = LS 22Q); again, past memories do not remove present bodily pain, but they can outweigh it.[8]

Bodily pleasures are fundamental for Epicurus, it seems, not in the sense that we should pursue them indiscriminately, but in that freedom from anxiety or *ataraxia*, itself a pleasure in the mind, is ultimately freedom from anxiety *about physical pain* – in the form of punishments in the afterlife, for example. This explains such passages as the following, which could on the face of it seem to be advocating gross physical indulgence:

> For I for my part cannot understand that good, if I remove those pleasures which are perceived by taste, those which are perceived in sex, those from listening to singing, those pleasant movements too which are received in the eyes from beautiful things, or any other pleasures which come about in the whole person through any of the senses. Nor can it be said that joy of the mind only is among good things, for I recognise a joyful mind by its hope that its nature will be in possession of all the things that I have mentioned above, and free from pain.
>
> (Epicurus cited by Cicero, *Tusculan Disputations* 3.41 = LS 21L)

I do not know how I can understand the good, if I remove the pleasures that come through taste and sex and hearing

and the pleasant movements caused in sight by beautiful shape.
(Epicurus cited by Athenaeus, 7.280A = Epicurus fr. 10 Bailey)

And, notoriously, 'The beginning and root of all good is the pleasure of the stomach; even wisdom and refinements (of culture) are to be referred to this' (Epicurus cited by Athenaeus, 12.546 = LS 21M). As Cicero makes his Epicurean spokesman say, recognition that mental pleasures and pains have their origin in bodily ones does not stop them being much greater than bodily ones (*On Ends* 1.55 = LS 21U). But one may still wonder whether Plutarch may not have some justification in complaining, in his essay *That a Pleasant life is not Possible by Following Epicurus*, that Epicureanism neglects the higher aspirations of the human spirit; and even within Epicurus' own doctrine it is difficult to see how the pleasure of remembering past philosophical discussions can be accommodated on this model, unless indeed the pleasurable thing about the discussions was just their removal of anxieties about the future. One fragment of Epicurus speaks of philosophy being distinctive in that enjoyment is present in the whole pursuit and not just at the end (*Vatican Sayings* 27 = LS 25I); but whether this implies that philosophy has value in itself, rather than as a means to the end of removing unfounded anxieties, and whether if so it entitles us to dismiss as rhetorical exaggeration the passages that imply that the value of philosophy *is* purely instrumental, is uncertain. (See in Chapter Two, on heavenly phenomena; also

If we were not troubled at all by misgivings about celestial phenomena, and misgivings that death might in some way be our concern, and also by not being aware of the limits of pains and desires, we would not stand in need of the study of nature. It is not possible to dispel fear about the most important things if one does not know what is the nature of the universe, but has some misgivings about the things in the myths. So it is not possible to enjoy pleasures in their purity without the study of nature.
(*PD* 11–12 = LS 25B)

The ancient sources draw a distinction between 'kinetic' pleasures, or pleasures involving change, on the one hand, and 'katastematic' or 'stationary' pleasures on the other; Epicurus, we are told, recognised both types with reference both to the body (or 'flesh') and the mind, unlike the rival Cyrenaic hedonist school which recognised only the kinetic pleasures of the body (DL 10.136 = LS 21R). The contrast has commonly been interpreted in the light of discussions of pleasure in Plato and Aristotle, as a contrast between (i) the pleasures involved in the process of change that removes a lack – drinking to satisfy thirst, for example – and (ii) the pleasure of simply not being subject to any lack, such as the pleasure of simply not being thirsty. Plato had in his *Gorgias* (493–4) symbolised two attitudes to pleasure by, on the one hand, a leaky jar that constantly needs to be refilled, and on the other a sound jar which needs little topping up; and he had made Socrates' opponent there, Callicles, describe the sort of existence suggested by the latter as like that of a corpse or a stone.

To interpret the contrast between kinetic and katastematic pleasures in this way seems natural in the context of the doctrine that the limit of pleasure is the removal of pain. But the pleasure of simply not being thirsty seems somewhat lacking in positive content, and open to the objection – made indeed by ancient critics: Cicero, *On Ends* 2.15ff. – that Epicurus is not really entitled to apply the same term 'pleasure' to the kinetic and katastematic types.

While Plato in writings after the *Gorgias* had continued to regard the pleasures of replenishment as inferior because of their necessary connection with pain, he had also argued that those who say that pleasure is nothing more than the absence of pain are mistaken (*Philebus* 44BC) and that there are other, superior pleasures not involving pain at all (ibid. 51–2, cf. *Republic* 9. 584–5). Aristotle's connection of pleasure with ongoing activity rather than with processes like that of replenishment makes a similar point (*EN* 10.3, cf. 7.12). For Epicurus too some have therefore suggested that katastematic pleasure is rather a positive sense of well-being that we enjoy when not subject to a lack. This could be connected with the fact that our soul and body atoms are, after all, in constant movement. (Since there is katastematic pleasure of the body as well as of the mind, we cannot argue that katastematic pleasure has positive content because it is just the *mental* pleasure of reflecting on the fact that the body is not subject to a lack.) Perhaps there is a positive pleasure in having one's atoms moving in harmonious patterns rather than being disrupted by some lack. Parallels have been seen with a text of Democritus which asserts that moderation brings 'good spirit' (*euthumiê*) and that deficiency and excess produce large movements which exclude this (KRS 594). But the interpretation of this passage in terms of atomic physical theory is controversial in Democritus (cf. KRS p. 432), let alone its extension to Epicurus.

Recently, however, Purinton has argued[9] that the parallel with Plato's and Aristotle's discussions of replenishment is misleading, and that kinetic pleasures are to be interpreted as including all pleasures which we directly experience as such; they may accompany the replenishment of a lack, but do not have to do so (though, as we have seen, once the lack is satisfied pleasure can only be varied and not increased). The role of katastematic pleasure, in Purinton's view, is essentially different, relating to the Epicurean point that in taking the long view, not pursuing any and every pleasure indiscriminately, we should not ignore – as the Cyrenaics did – the fact that not being in pain, even if it does not positively *feel* pleasant in itself, is a good not to be disregarded, and one which may even lead us to endure a lesser pain now for the sake of avoiding a greater one in the future. A life could not indeed be katastematically pleasant without *some* kinetic pleasures – pleasure is something which living creatures need;[10] but getting this *particular* kinetic pleasure rather than that is less important than the overall katastematic pleasure of a life founded on the principle that the removal of pain is the limit of pleasure.

Moral virtue will play a part in freedom from anxiety. The person who is unjust will be beset by anxieties which will destroy his or her peace of mind, as we shall see in Chapter Six. Cicero indeed suggests that virtue's relation to pleasure for Epicurus is purely as a means to an end, and finds this shocking, citing the Stoic Cleanthes' critical description of the virtues as Pleasure's servants (*On Ends* 2.69 = LS 21O). Other passages suggest that acting virtuously is pleasant in itself;[11] virtue will still, however, derive its *value* from pleasure, which is the sole good, rather than constituting an independent good.

The anxieties which according to Epicurus and Lucretius most trouble people stem from two fears: from fear of divine wrath, and from fear of death which, whether we realise it or not, creates our desire for the wrong sort of security and is thus a major cause of wrongdoing:

The principal anxiety in human souls comes about through

thinking that [the heavenly bodies] are blessed and indestructible, and yet have wishes and act and cause things to come about in a way that is inconsistent with this; and in always expecting some eternal terror or being apprehensive of what is in the myths, or also being fearful of the very loss of sensation in death, as if it applied to themselves . . .

(*ad Hdt.* 81)

Against the fear of death Epicurus' and Lucretius' basic argument is simple: since we do not exist after death, it is no concern to us: 'Death is nothing to us; for what has been dissolved is without sensation, and what is without sensation is nothing to us' (*PD* 2). Stories of torments in the underworld are therefore false and should cause us no fear.

This, however, is open to a double objection. First of all, it may be questioned – and is questioned by critics of Epicureanism in Cicero's dialogues – whether fears of punishment in the afterlife were really as widespread as Epicurus, and especially Lucretius, make out. May they not to some extent be creating a target just in order to attack it? 'What old woman is so stupid as to fear those things which you allegedly would fear if you had not learnt natural science?' (Cicero, *Tusculan Disputations* 1.48; cf. *On the Nature of the Gods* 1.86, 2.5).

To this there may be two replies. First, Lucretius argues that people's claims that they are not affected by superstitious fears should not be believed, especially when they say one thing in times of prosperity but behave in quite a different way in times of adversity (the 'churches are fuller in wartime' argument: 3.48ff.). Second, as with fear of the heavenly bodies as divine, Epicurus at least may be aiming his polemic against a specific target: Plato's writings, and here his myths of retribution in the afterlife.

Nevertheless, the suspicion of attacking the wrong target remains; for people's fear of death may be not fear of existing after death in some unpleasant circumstances, but fear of annihilation itself. As Seneca puts it,

> Even when you are persuaded that those are fables and that those who have died have nothing more to fear, another apprehension arises; for people are afraid not only that they will be in the underworld, but also that they will be – nowhere.

(Seneca, *Letters on Morals* 82.16)

Here the best that Epicurus or Lucretius can offer is, first, the claim that it is pointless to worry about the prospect of something that will not trouble us when it is actually present (*ad Men*. 125 = LS 24A), and, second, an argument from the analogy with the past: the thought that there was a time in the past when we did not exist does not cause us any anxiety, so why should the corresponding thought about the future?

> Again, consider how the endless ages that elapsed before we were born are nothing to us. Thus nature shows us this as a mirror of the time that will be after we have finally died. Surely nothing appears there to shudder at, surely nothing seems gloomy; is it not more free from care than any sleep?
>
> (Lucretius, 3.972ff.)

But to this the natural reply is that our attitudes to the past and the future in general are not the same, and that the threat of future ills quite generally causes us more anxiety than the memory of past ones; or, putting it another way, that human beings have natural desires concerning future projects which death as annihilation seems to threaten. And we may not all find much consolation in the thought that, however long we may live, we will still be dead for an infinite length of time after that (ibid. 3.1087 = LS 24G). Perhaps to unchanging gods – Aristotelian, or even Epicurean? – past and future are alike; and Epicurus claims that by following his philosophy we can be like the gods. But he may, as Martha Nussbaum in particular has forcefully argued, be disregarding what makes human life distinctively human.[12]

Lucretius ends his third book with a whole series of arguments against the fear of death. Where he may seem to be on stronger ground is when he is in fact arguing, though without himself explicitly distinguishing the two points, not so much that death is not to be feared as that to be preoccupied with the fear of death achieves nothing except to ruin the life you already have. Some of his arguments may seem to beg the question, as is natural enough in what is, after all, rhetorical exhortation verging on satire, rather than dispassionate philosophical argument. Thus he likens the person who fears death to a guest at a banquet (3.935ff.; the image is taken up by Horace, *Satires* 1.1.117–19), and presents Nature personified as saying that if life has been satisfactory one should be content to leave it, if unsatisfactory one should not wish to prolong it:

For if your past life has been pleasant for you, and all its benefits have not, as if poured into a leaky vessel, run out and perished without being enjoyed, why do you not retire satisfied by the banquet of life, and with a calm spirit accept rest free from care, you fool? But if whatever you have enjoyed has been wasted and come to nothing and your life is a burden to you, why do you seek to add more which will in turn perish and come to nothing without being enjoyed; why do you not rather make an end both of life and of trouble? For there is nothing further that I can discover or contrive to please you; all things are always the same.

(Lucretius, 3.935ff.)

One might object that a third case has not been taken into account, that of the person who has lived an unsatisfactory and unhappy life so far but could reform and achieve at least some time of happiness (by adopting Epicureanism) if given more time to do it in.

Both Epicurus and Lucretius claim that pleasure is not increased by being prolonged – in effect, that it is quality of life that matters rather than quantity. Longer life may give you the same pleasure for more time; it cannot, if you have achieved the most pleasurable life that is humanly possible, bring any *greater degree* of pleasure:

Infinite and finite time contain equal pleasure, if one measures the limits [of pleasure] by reason. The flesh takes the limits of pleasure to be unlimited, and pleasure [as requiring] unlimited time to provide it. But the mind, having understood the goal and the limits of the flesh, and removed fears concerning eternity, provides us with a life that is complete, and we no longer need unlimited time; [the mind] neither avoids pleasure nor, when circumstances are making ready our departure from life, does it come to its end as if it lacked anything from the best life.

(PD 19–20 = LS 24C; cf. Lucretius, 3.1081)

This, however, raises the question: does Epicurus, in his anxiety to dispel the fear of death, not risk suggesting that there is nothing to choose between living for another twenty years with the maximum happiness possible for a human being, on the one hand, and dying tomorrow, on the other?[13] May Epicurus and Lucretius not end up by presenting existence and non-existence as alternatives between which there really is not much to choose, playing down the joys of life in order to make us less reluctant to relinquish it? Not that Epicurus advocates suicide, except in extreme circumstances; if your life is such that you do not want to continue it, it is your own fault for living in a way that has made it so, and indeed it is paradoxically often the fear of death that produces the anxieties that drive people to suicide. (Cf. Epicurus cited by Seneca, *Letters on Morals* 24.22.)

When Lucretius insists that we should not spoil the life we have by anxiety about our death, which is inevitable anyway, he surely has a point. Nature's speech, quoted above, continues, to the person who complains at the prospect of death even though already old,

> Away with your tears, clown, and check your complaints. Having enjoyed all life's rewards, now you are in decline. *But because you have always desired what you do not have, and despised what is there for the taking, your life has slipped away, incomplete and without being enjoyed,* and death stands unexpectedly beside you before you can depart from your affairs replete and satisfied.
>
> (Lucretius, 3.955ff.; my emphasis)

Enjoying the present is in fact the genuine Epicurean version of the 'popular Epicureanism' enshrined in the injunction to 'eat, drink and be merry, for tomorrow we die'. But the popular notion often carries with it overtones of anxiety which are quite un-Epicurean, as in Horace:

> Tell them to bring here wine and perfume and the flowers of the lovely rose which do not last, while circumstances and your age and the black threads spun by the three Fates still allow.
>
> (Horace, *Odes* 2.3.13–16)

> While we speak, jealous time is flying past; enjoy the present day, trusting as little as possible in tomorrow.
>
> (ibid. 1.11.7–8)

The genuine Epicurean will indeed enjoy life (frugally, for the most part) because it is the only opportunity for enjoyment we have. But he or she will do so with due regard for the future consequences of present actions (since, presumably, although we *may* not be alive tomorrow, we probably will be, and should not risk a greater pain then for the sake of a lesser pleasure now, or avoid a lesser pain now if it will save us from a greater one tomorrow), and without being anxious or preoccupied with the thought of death. Lucretius describes in terms which are not without some present-day echoes the dissatisfaction – we would call it neurotic anxiety or alienation – which is, in his view, prompted by the fear of death, whether we realise this or not:

> We see people for the most part not knowing what they want for themselves and always seeking a change of place as if they could cast off a burden. The great man often goes out of his lofty doors, when he is bored with being at home, and swiftly <comes back> since he feels no better outside; he drives his expensive ponies headlong to his country house, as if hurrying to save a house on fire; he starts yawning as soon as he crosses the threshold, and either falls into a deep sleep and seeks oblivion, or again hurries to get back to the city. In this way everyone is running away from himself, but unwillingly he is stuck to and hates the one whom, as it turns out, he cannot escape, because in his sickness he does not grasp the cause of the disease . . .
>
> (Lucretius, 3.1057-70)

Modern sensibilities tend to regard Lucretius as callous when he writes

> 'Now your happy home will no longer welcome you, or your good wife, and your sweet children will not run to meet you and snatch the first kiss and touch your heart with silent sweetness. You will not be able to prosper in your affairs and protect your family. Alas, alas,' they say, 'one unhappy day has completely taken away from you so many rewards of life.' *But what they do not add in these circumstances is 'and now you don't miss any of these things any longer'.*
>
> (ibid. 3.894ff. = LS 24E: my emphasis)

We suppose that we *ought* to be distressed at the thought that after death we will not be able to protect our families (an even more important matter, indeed, in ancient conditions of social organisation than in modern); and we may resent the fact that Lucretius first shows us a picture of domestic happiness, unusual enough in Roman literature, and then deflates it. Indeed, if he is speaking of someone who dies relatively young, with children not yet grown to adulthood, and who is unable to look after the family when one might naturally expect that one would, then we may be justified in finding his attitude callous; but, like it or not, for all of us, if we do not suffer the misfortune of our children predeceasing us, there will come a time when we will have to leave them to their own devices and will no longer be around to influence them. *And since this is inevitable, the Epicurean message goes, we will be happier if we do like it than if we don't.* For the Epicurean as for the Stoic, happiness lies in accepting the inevitable. The paradox is that the Epicurean, who believes that each person's attitudes to events and situations are not predetermined, adopts what most would see as a more passive approach to life, while the Stoic, who believes that each person's attitudes are predetermined, adopts a more active one, as we shall see.

Most telling of all, perhaps, in the context of the Epicurean atomic theory, is the argument that we should accept our death because the everlasting atoms of which we, body and soul alike, are made are needed for reuse – for recycling, in the modern jargon. Lucretius addresses the person who is reluctant to die:

> There is need for matter for future generations to grow, and yet they will all follow you when they have finished with life; just so before now generations have perished no less than you, and so they will continue to do. Thus one thing never ceases to spring up from another; no one is granted life as a freehold, but everyone has a temporary lease of it.
>
> (ibid. 3.967–71 = LS 24F)

It may seem to the reader that the discussion of Epicurean ethics in this chapter has devoted excessive space to the question of the fear of death. The justification for this is twofold. We are, first of all, constrained by the actual state of our sources, and Lucretius develops this particular theme at length. But second and more importantly, Lucretius' discussion of the fear of death provides us with an extended context in which we can see what Epicurean ethical attitudes amount to in practice – though we should remember that Lucretius is in this section drawing not just on Epicurean sources but on themes of popular moralising in general, and on the literary genre of consolation to the bereaved in particular.

THE STOICS

Plato had made Socrates argue that a wicked person cannot be happy, however prosperous that person is in worldly terms. But he does not make him explicitly argue the converse, that a virtuous person will be happy just by being virtuous, regardless of the material circumstances. Plato's Socrates is challenged (*Republic* 2.361) to show only that the righteous person who is being tortured is happier than the wicked person who is prosperous, not that he or she is happy *tout court*. And Aristotle for his part describes the claim that a person who is suffering the greatest misfortune is happy as one that no one would defend who was not arguing for the sake of argument (*EN* 1.5 1096a1; cf. 7.13 1153b19) – though he nevertheless suggests that a virtuous person cannot ever be truly wretched, either. (*EN* 1.10 1101a34; we will have occasion to return to this passage later.) In his *Rhetoric* (1.5 1360b14ff.; adopting a more popular view to suit the context, but cf. also *EN* 1.8 1099b3) Aristotle regards happiness as including wealth, good children, health, honour and much else besides; later writers picked out his follower Theophrastus as 'weakening' virtue by claiming that it was not sufficient for happiness (Cicero, *Tusculan Disputations* 5.24; *Academica* 1.33ff.).

They did so because they required a view to contrast with that of the Stoics. For the Stoics did hold that virtue or wisdom (the two being equated) is sufficient in itself for happiness (DL 7.127 = LS 61I; Cicero, *Tusculan Disputations* 5.82 = LS 63M), and that virtue alone is good, wickedness alone evil (DL 7.102 = LS 58A). Where others might say that virtue was so important that no other considerations could outweigh it or come anywhere near doing so – so that between virtue plus poverty and wickedness plus riches there is no real contest – the Stoics went further and denied that riches and virtue could enter into the same calculation at all; in judging what is good our only concern should be to behave virtuously:

> Indeed, if wisdom [i.e. virtue] and wealth were both *desirable*, the combination of both would be more desirable than wisdom alone; but it is not the case that, if both are *deserving of approbation*, the combination is worth more than wisdom alone on its own. For we judge health deserving of a certain degree of approbation but do not place it among goods, and we consider that there is no degree of approbation so great

that it can be preferred to virtue. This the Peripatetics do not hold, for they must say that an action which is both virtuous and without pain is more desirable than the same action accompanied by pain. We [Stoics] think otherwise.

(Cicero, *On Ends* 3.44; my emphasis)

Virtuous behaviour, however, needs to be defined. For the Cynics virtue consisted in 'living according to nature', and Zeno, the founder of the Stoic school, who had been a pupil of the Cynic Crates before founding his own school, took over this definition; his successors modified the formulation but preserved its essence (Stobaeus, *Selections* 2.7.6a, p. 75.11ff. Wachsmuth–Hense, DL 7.87–9 = LS 63BC). For the Cynics it seems that 'life according to nature' was largely a negative slogan, involving the rejection of conventional ways of behaving;[14] but for Zeno and for orthodox Stoics after him it had positive content, indicating that we should live in accordance with our own human nature, and also with the nature of the universe of which we are parts. No human being, not even the Stoic sage, can foresee everything that the future – which is to say, fate and providence – has in store; since our knowledge is limited we should follow the guidance of our own nature, but if things turn out otherwise we should accept this as for the best (Chapter Four).

What, then, is the guidance of our own nature? Where Epicurus claimed that the first instinct of any new-born living creature was for pleasure, the Stoics claimed that it was for self-preservation (DL 7.85–6 = LS 57A). The instinct for self-preservation is described in terms of the creature's 'appropriation' to itself – its recognition of its body, first of all, as its own. 'Appropriation', *oikeiôsis*, is a term with no very natural English equivalent; its force can perhaps be more easily grasped by contrasting it with its more familiar opposite, 'alienation'.[15] Significantly, for the Stoics it is usually a matter of us being appropriated to things by nature, rather than appropriating them to ourselves. Bulls are instinctively aware of their horns (Hierocles, *Elements of Ethics* 2.5 = LS 57C); a tortoise placed on its back struggles to right itself, and endures pain in order to do so (Seneca, *Letters on Morals* 121.8 = LS 57B) – the point presumably being that if the animal could calculate it might be trading off present pain for future pleasure, but if it cannot it must be instinct that drives it to strive for its natural condition. As Long and Sedley stress (p. 352) the appeal to nature is not intended to imply that we should behave in a certain way because animals do so; rather, observation of animals can help to reinforce our understanding of what is natural for us and for them, and to refute the Epicureans.

As the infant human being grows and develops, its 'appropriation' develops in two ways; it comes to recognise more fully what its own nature involves, and it builds links with other human beings, in its family, its city and so on (DL 7.86 = LS 57A). The latter aspect we will return to in Chapter Six. A human being thus comes to recognise that it is natural to pursue certain things and avoid others; health and wealth, for example, will fall in the first group, sickness and poverty in the latter. Ordinary people think that these are respectively goods and evils; but the person who eventually comes to be a Stoic sage will realise that they are not (Cicero, *On Ends* 3.21 = LS 59D). For one's own true nature, what really matters is one's reason; virtue, the only good, consists in making the right selections (not choices, for virtue alone is worthy of *choice*) among external and bodily goods and in attempting to put one's selections into effect as far as one can. This is in our own individual control; whether we succeed is not, and is irrelevant to our happiness.

Virtue alone is good; health and wealth are indifferent, but they fall into a class of 'preferred indifferents'. Wealth is preferred as a means to an end – it can be used to perform virtuous actions; bodily fitness, however, is preferred both for this reason and for its own sake, because it is natural (DL 7.107; cf. LS vol. 2, p. 355). Sickness and poverty are 'unpreferred indifferents'; that is to say, we should try to avoid them if we can do so without compromising our virtue (we should not steal to pay the doctor's bill, for example), but what is important is that we behave rationally, i.e. virtuously, by *trying* to avoid them, not that we should succeed in doing so. Other things of no importance at all, such as having an odd or even number of hairs, are indifferents that are neither preferred nor unpreferred (DL 7.104 = LS 58B). One early Stoic, Aristo of Chios, rejected the notion of preferred and unpreferred indifferents, arguing that everything except virtue and wickedness was, simply, indifferent; but by adopting this view he risked denying virtue its content and returning to the Cynic position. Cicero indeed compares Aristo to Pyrrho (*On Ends* 2.43 = LS 2G, 3.50 = LS 58I), but Aristo denied only differences in value in things other than virtue and vice themselves, while Pyrrho's scepticism extended to all determinable differences in anything whatsoever.

The Stoic Diogenes of Babylon in the second century BC defined the purpose of life as 'to act in accordance with good reason in the selection and rejection of the things that are in accordance with nature', and his successor Antipater as 'to live selecting what is in accordance with nature and rejecting what is contrary to nature continuously' (Stobaeus, *Selections* 2.7.6a, p. 76.9ff. Wachsmuth–Hense = LS 58K). Antipater also defined the goal as 'to do everything as far as oneself is concerned continuously and undeviatingly with a view to obtaining the primary things in accordance with nature' (ibid.). (Presumably it is implied 'so long as one does not act immorally in doing so'; or perhaps this is taken care of by virtue itself being in accordance with nature.)

Antipater's second formulation brings out more clearly the implication that the goal is to try to obtain things in accordance with nature rather than actually to obtain them:

> See then what results for them, that the end is to act reasonably in the selection of things that have value for acting reasonably. For they say that they do not have or conceive of any other essence of the good or of happiness than this much-honoured reasonableness in the selection of things that have value. – But there are those who think that this is said against Antipater rather than against the [whole] sect; for he entered into these ingenious arguments under pressure from Carneades.
>
> (Plutarch, *CN* 1072EF = LS 64D)

Critics like Plutarch found the implication that it is selection that is important, rather than the things selected, absurd. But there is nothing in these later formulations alien to Chrysippus' own doctrines, even if – probably in reaction to Academic criticisms, as Plutarch indicates – they bring out the distinctive features of the Stoic position all the more clearly. The Stoic sage is like an archer whose goal is not to hit the target, but to do the best he can to hit the target:

> All appropriate acts can rightly be said to relate to this purpose, that we may obtain the primary things of nature – not, however, that this is the ultimate good; for virtuous action is not among the primary natural attractions; it is a

consequence and arises later, as I have said.... No one should think that it follows that there are two ultimate goods. For we speak of the ultimate good as if someone's purpose was to aim a spear or arrow at something; the man in the example would have to do everything he could to aim straight. That he should *do* everything to achieve his purpose would be, as it were, his ultimate good, as we speak of the supreme good in life; but that he should *hit* the mark is as it were be selected, but not to be desired.

(Cicero, On Ends 3.22 = LS 59D, 64F)

Plutarch attacks this image too (*CN* 1071A = LS 64C); but is it not true that no archer, however good, can guarantee that a stray gust of wind will not throw his arrow off course?

The Stoics are certainly not, as Plutarch also suggests, trapped in a circular argument defining virtue in terms of what we should pursue and what we should pursue in terms of virtue:

> They posit, as the essence of the good, the reasonable selection of the things in accordance with nature; but selection is not reasonable if it is not with a view to some end, as was stated above. What, then, is this [end]? Nothing other, they say, than acting reasonably in the selection of the things in accordance with nature. First of all, the notion of the good is gone and disappeared; for... being compelled to derive our notion of being reasonable from the end, and to think of the end not apart from this, we fail to think of either.

(Plutarch, CN 1072C)

The argument is not circular, in spite of Plutarch's objections, for it is *nature* that defines what we should pursue, even though it is the pursuit itself rather than the things pursued that are the true end. With more justice, perhaps, critics also protested that the Stoic account of human development contained a sudden break, leaving human nature behind; the transition from being on the way to virtue to having actually achieved it involves realising that the things one thought good in themselves are not in fact so.

> But what is there less consistent than their saying that, when they have discovered the supreme good, they go back to nature and look for the principle of action – that is, of appropriate action – from her? For it is not the thought of action or appropriate action that impels us to desire those

things which are in accordance with nature; rather, both desire and action are aroused by those things.

(Cicero, *On Ends* 4.48)

Panaetius was, however, able to give a detailed and not implausible account of how the four cardinal virtues of Greek thought – wisdom, justice, bravery and moderation respectively – arise from natural instincts:

Everything which is right arises from one of four parts [sc. of our natural instincts]; it is either concerned with perception of truth and expert skill; or with the preservation of human society, the assignment to each person of their due and faithfulness in undertakings; or with the greatness and strength of a lofty and unconquered spirit; or with order and moderation in all things that are said and done, this constituting modesty and self-control.

(Cicero, *On Duties* 1.15)

The Stoic sage, and the ordinary person who is doing what he or she should, will make the same selections – e.g., in most circumstances, health rather than sickness, wealth rather than poverty – and will try to put them into effect. The difference is in their attitude and motivation. For the ordinary person thinks that it is achieving health that matters, while the Stoic sage will realise that the important thing is trying to do so. A precisely similar action will be a *kathêkon* (a fitting, or appropriate action; the word that Cicero translated by *officium*, duty) whoever performs it, but a *katorthôma*, a correct action, if and only if performed by a sage. (Strictly, it will be a *meson kathêkon* if performed by somebody other than a sage, Stobaeus, *Selections* 2.7.8, p. 86.2 Wachsmuth–Hense = LS 59B). The Stoics recognised, indeed, that what is fitting will in many cases depend upon the particular circumstances; some actions, such as sacrificing one's property, are appropriate only in particular circumstances.[16]

The sage's virtue consists in possession not just of individual true judgements but of *truth* – a systematic body of moral knowledge. Virtue cannot therefore be easily lost – or so one might expect, though in fact there was a debate within the school over whether virtue could be lost, by senility or, more oddly, through the sage's getting drunk (DL 7.127 = LS 61I). There is no middle ground between virtue and wickedness, wisdom and folly; though some people who are not virtuous are 'making progress' (*prokoptontes*) towards virtue, everyone who is not wise and virtuous is mad and bad (Plutarch, *SR* 31 1048E; Alexander of Aphrodisias, *On Fate* 28 199.14 = LS 61N):

> Whoever is driven blindly along by evil stupidity and ignorance of the truth, him the porch and herd of Chrysippus declares to be insane. This rule applies to all nations and to great kings, to everyone except the wise.
>
> (Horace, *Satires* 2.3.43ff.)

Any falling short of the ideal is a falling short; one can drown just as well half a yard below the surface as at the bottom of the sea (Plutarch, *CN* 1063A = LS 61T). The Stoics thus insisted that all wrong actions were equal (Stobaeus, *Selections* 2.7.11o, p. 113.18 Wachsmuth–Hense = LS 59O); this is a deliberate paradox – true from one point of view, false from another – which incurred the derision of their critics:

> Nor will this principle prevail, that the fault is equal and the same of the person who breaks off young cabbages in someone else's garden and of the one who at night carries off the sacred emblems of the gods.[17] Let there be a rule to demand punishments that fit the crimes, so that you do not use the terrible scourge on what only deserves the whip.
>
> (Horace, *Satires* 1.3.115ff.)

And indeed the very passage of Stobaeus just cited allows that, even if all wrong actions are equally wrong, there is a difference between those that result from inveterate wickedness and those that do not. The latter will presumably include the inevitable mistakes made by the *prokoptontes*.

Not surprisingly, the Stoic sage is as rare as the phoenix (Alexander of Aphrodisias, loc. cit.); and Chrysippus did not claim that either he himself or any of his teachers or acquaintances was a sage (Plutarch, *SR* 31 1048E). The final change to virtue when you become a sage is so slight you do not notice it (ibid.). Since death is not in itself an evil, suicide may sometimes be the rational, and therefore virtuous, course to follow (Cicero, *On Ends* 3.60–1 = LS 66G; DL 7.130 = LS 66H). Seneca in particular – perhaps because of his personal situation under Nero – lays great emphasis on suicide as the guarantee of personal freedom, but is perhaps unorthodox in the extent to which he does so.

Modern criticism of Stoic ethics has centred on the seeming inhumanity of the Stoic sage. The objection is well illustrated by the example, not found in this form in ancient sources but reconstructed according to Stoic principles, of the Stoic sage who comes home to find the house on fire and his child inside. (I take the example from Long, *Hellenistic Philosophy* 197–8.) If there is any possibility of saving the child, the Stoic sage will try to do so. (It would be foolhardy, and so not virtuous, to try if there was no hope; it would be failing to act in accordance with nature not to try to save the child if there was any hope of doing so.) But the sage will try to save the child *not*, ultimately, from concern about saving the child, but from concern to do the right thing. And if the sage is beaten back by the flames and the child dies, there will be no regrets – and that, it would seem, for three reasons. First, because the sage did the right thing; that is what being a Stoic sage, and hence virtuous, *means*, and hence it is a logically demonstrable truth that a sage will have no regrets. Saving the child was not in the sage's power; trying to save it was, and that the sage did. Second, death is not an evil but an 'unpreferred indifferent', so nothing really bad has happened either to the child or to the sage himself (Anaxagoras, in the fifth century BC, when he heard of his son's death, said that he knew he had begotten a mortal (Cicero, *Tusculan Disputations* 3.30) and Epictetus said that, if you kiss your wife, you should be aware she is a mortal (*Discourses* 1.1.22)). And third, everything that happens is ordered for the best by Providence, even if we cannot understand how. It would not be alien to Stoic thought to argue that the apparent disaster has given the sage an opportunity to put virtue into practice, both in trying to save the child and in not grieving afterwards, and also that it may have forestalled some real evil for the child if not for the sage (i.e. it may have been destined that the child would grow up to be wicked).

The Stoic attitude may seem harsh, even repulsive. But we should note two things: first, that as far as actions are concerned the Stoic sage acts in just the same way as anyone else, and tries just as hard to save the child; if that is the proper thing to do, it would not be virtuous to do otherwise. Second, the Stoic distinction between what is in our power and what is not has a point. The Stoics certainly push the importance of intentions, as opposed to results, to paradoxical extremes, like so much else in their doctrine; we should beware of watering down the paradoxes in order to make the Stoic position seem more acceptable, but equally we should not disregard what there is to be said in its favour. The claim that virtue alone is good can be seen as an attempt to stress the distinction between moral and non-moral values; the implication that it is not only more in our own self-interest to be unjustly tortured than to do wrong, but that we will be just as happy in those circumstances as if we were virtuous and prosperous, may seem bizarre, but is it any more so than the belief that we should do our duty regardless of the consequences, or the belief that we should act for the greatest happiness of the greatest number even if that does not include ourselves?[18]

Panaetius, though not rejecting any of the traditional positions of orthodox Stoic ethics, laid emphasis on the situation of those progressing to virtue, rather than on the ideal of the sage, unrealised in practice; he also drew a distinction between four ethical *personae* – the term originally meaning 'mask' – to be taken into account in assessing the duties of each individual:

> One must understand that we are, as it were, endowed by nature with two *personae*; one of these is common as a result of the fact that we all share in reason and the superiority that it gives us over the beasts; it is from this that all that is right and fitting derives, and it is starting from this that we inquire rationally about our duty; the second is that which is assigned to individuals as proper to them .... To the two *personae* which I mentioned above is added a third, imposed by some chance or circumstance, and also a fourth, which we ourselves adopt by our own decision.
>
> (Cicero, *On Duties* 1.107, 115 = LS 66E)

And – although Panaetius is careful to say that we should not go against universal nature, of which more later – it is our own particular nature that we should follow:

> But each person must hold altogether to his own: not to his vices, but to what is proper to him, so that the fittingness [in actions] which we are seeking may more easily be maintained. For we must act in such a way that we do not at all strive against universal nature, but, while observing this, follow our own proper nature; accordingly, even if there are other things which are more weighty and better, nevertheless we should measure our pursuits by the rule of our own

proper nature. For there is no use in fighting against nature
or in pursuing anything which you cannot achieve.

(ibid. 1.110 = LS 66E)

Antiochus of Ascalon, Cicero's teacher, rejected Academic scepticism, as we saw in Chapter Two, and argued that there had been
a single ancient dogmatic philosophy, the essentials of which were
shared by Plato, Aristotle and the Stoics (Cicero, *Academica*
1.24ff., 1.43), though he did recognise certain features of Stoic
doctrine as distinctive – the goodness of virtue alone, the placing
of all the virtues in reason, the denial that the sage has passions,
the rejection of (Aristotle's) fifth heavenly element, the doctrine
of the apprehensive impression and the consequent belief that the
senses were (sometimes) trustworthy (ibid. 1.35–42). Even so, as
a historical reconstruction Antiochus' single 'ancient philosophy'
makes earlier dogmatic philosophies more alike than they really
were, though from his perspective it was not inappropriate to
group these three schools together and contrast them both with
the Epicureans and with the Academic sceptics, and we cannot
rule out the possibility that Antiochus' conception of dogmatic
Platonism may be more appropriate to Plato's Academy in the
time of Polemo, the fourth head of the school and teacher of
the Stoic Zeno, than to Plato himself.

Antiochus argued that virtue alone was sufficient for the happy
life, but virtue plus external goods would produce 'the happiest'
life (Cicero, *Tusculan Disputations* 5.21–3, *Academica* 1.22).[19] But
against Antiochus it was rightly objected that happiness is by
definition a limit; you cannot be *too* happy (Cicero, *On Ends*
5.81). And as soon as one allows that external goods make a
difference – that they really *are* goods – how is it possible any
more to claim that one can still be happy without them (Cicero,
Tusculan Disputations 5.23)? Antiochus indeed claims that they
make only a very small difference (Cicero, *On Ends* 5.71, 5.91);
but he is pretty clearly trying to have it both ways. Annas has
shown (420) how Antiochus' position might be seen as an interpretation, one still sometimes advanced today but in fact wrong, of a
passage in Aristotle's *EN* (1.10 1101a6) which might give the false
impression that 'blessedness' is regarded as a higher degree of
happiness than happiness itself. Arius Didymus, the court philosopher of the emperor Augustus, understood Aristotle's position
more accurately (Annas 415–18).

Cicero criticises the Stoic position by arguing that the sage would choose virtue plus external 'goods' rather than virtue alone, if given the choice (Cicero, *On Ends* 4.59; cf. Alexander of Aphrodisias, *Supplement to the Book* On the Soul 163.4ff.). The problem is, however, misconceived; since virtue is defined in terms of making the right selection among external things, then on any given occasion either it will be proper to try to get the external things, or not. The question whether the virtuous person tries to get them because of some extra happiness they bring simply does not arise.

Aristotle had argued that external goods were needed as resources for virtue (*EN* 1.8 = 1099a31); but the Stoic notion of virtue is different from Aristotle's, and Stoic virtue can be practised even by a slave – it is a matter of making the right selections in the situation in which you find yourself, even if your power to achieve anything in material terms is restricted. There are texts which suggest that Panaetius and Posidonius allowed preferred indifferents the status of goods (DL 7.103, 128; LS vol. 2, p. 404); but even Chrysippus had been prepared to accept this as a loose use of words (Plutarch, *SR* 30 1048A = LS 58H), and Seneca (*Letters on Morals* 87.35 = F170 EK) reports Posidonius as arguing that wealth and health are not goods. When the notoriously inaccurate bishop Epiphanius quotes Posidonius as saying 'that the greatest good among human beings was wealth and health' (*Against Heresies* 3.2.9) we need not suppose that Posidonius endorsed this opinion himself.

Stoic moral theory, with its emphasis (at least until Panaetius) on the practically unrealisable figure of the sage, may seem hopelessly idealistic. But it may be important to remember that, as was stressed at the start of the present chapter, the emphasis in ancient ethics was on the sort of person one should be, rather than on the right way to behave in a given situation. The Stoic sage may be an unattainable ideal for what a human being may be like; but perhaps ideals ought not to be too easily attainable. We may think that the Stoic sage is not the sort of person we should even want to try to be, but that is another issue.

As we saw in Chapter Three, Panaetius questioned belief in divination and rejected that in the periodic conflagration of the world. This, together with his emphasis on the types of human character, may suggest a shift from thought about the universe as a whole to specifically human concerns;[20] and it is clear that his

concerns were more narrowly centred on the practicalities of ethics
than those of earlier Stoics. We are told that Panaetius drew a
distinction between practical and theoretical virtue (DL 7.92), but
no further detail is given.

There is, however, a more general question: whatever Panaetius'
actual position, *can* Stoic ethical theory be detached from its context in Stoic physics and remain coherent? Annas has argued
(159ff., 176ff.) that the cosmic context was not important for early
Stoic ethics, and that it is the later, Roman Stoics in particular who
stress the idea of each human being as a part of a greater whole.
The latter point is certainly true, and we will see some striking
examples in Chapter Seven. But the image of the dog tied to the
wagon is attributed to Zeno and Chrysippus (p. 77), and Chrysippus also said

> As long as what will follow is not clear to me, I always cling
> to the things better suited by nature for obtaining the things
> in accordance with nature; for God himself gave me the
> power of selecting these. But if I knew that it was fated for
> me to be ill now, I would eagerly seek that; for the foot too,
> if it had sense, would eagerly seek to be covered with mud.
> (Chrysippus cited by Epictetus, *Discourses* 2.6.9f. = LS 58J)

This suggests that the cosmic context was important for the early
Stoa too. Annas asks (162) what happiness there can be in con-
forming to an external standard; but it is important to recognise,
first that the standard is not for the Stoics a purely external one,
for each human being is part of the larger system, and second that
the Stoics are not claiming that submissiveness is a virtue in itself,
regardless of what one is submitting to.

There is, however, a distinction to be drawn. The Stoics, both
early and late, may indeed introduce a cosmic aspect into ethics by
holding that one should accept the failure of one's own attempts, as
being in the interests of a greater whole. But Annas is right to
stress that early Stoic ethical theory – and later Stoic theory too,
for that matter – does not base on non-human nature its claims
about what course of action is natural for a human being, about
what we ought to *try* to achieve. There is no theoretical difficulty
in claiming that human nature should guide our actions, without
any reference to the ordering of the universe as a whole. The link
(not confined to the Stoics) between human reason and the divine
no doubt makes it *easier* to argue that reason is the most important

human characteristic, but it is not essential to that argument; Aristotle too believes in the divinity of reason, but he does not appeal to it in the first book of the *EN*. What is more problematic is whether specifically Stoic ethics, and the claim that outcomes do not matter and the sage should therefore have no regrets, can be maintained in the absence of a belief that everything in the world happens for the best even if we cannot understand how. Could one adopt the Stoic view of virtue, and of human nature, and above all of *happiness*, in an essentially hostile and unfriendly world – an Epicurean one, for example? And could one do so in the absence *both* of any belief in personal immortality (which the Stoics did not accept, in the sense of an everlasting existence) *and* of belief that our selves, even if not everlasting, are ultimately parts of a greater whole?

Some passages from Marcus Aurelius in Chapter Seven will direct us to this question again. Meanwhile, we may note that the idea that we are parts of a greater whole is not absent even in Epicureanism, in Lucretius' 'recycling' argument for example (above, p. 99); and the emphasis in his poem on the perishability of all compounds, even our whole world, and the vastness of the infinite universe may in a way provide the human beings who observe and describe it with a sort of vicarious significance:

So the lively power of [Epicurus'] mind won through, and he travelled far beyond the fiery walls of the world, and traversed the whole immensity of space in mind and spirit, and in triumph brought back to us reports of what can happen and what cannot, in short of the principle by which the power of each thing is determined and a deep-set boundary-stone fixed for it.

(Lucretius, 1.72–6)

As soon as your [Epicurus'] reasoning, arising from your divine mind, begins to tell of the nature of things, the terrors of my mind flee away, the walls of the world part, and I see the processes taking place throughout the whole of space . . . . then at these things a certain divine pleasure and shuddering awe seizes upon me, because by your power nature is so openly revealed and made apparent on all sides.

(ibid., 3.14–30)

First look at the sea, the lands and the sky; their threefold

nature, these three bodies, Memmius, three things so different
in appearance, three compounds woven together in such ways
– all will be consigned to destruction by one single day, and
the massive mechanism of the world, maintained through
many years, will fall apart.

(ibid., 5.92–6)

But in the first two passages cited Lucretius' concern is more with
the benefits for mankind of Epicurus' discoveries, and the cosmic
perspective is hardly a central Epicurean idea except in so far as
it points up the importance of one's life here and now by contrast.
Your lifetime, however long or short it may turn out to be, is all
you have to experience and to make the best of, in a scheme of
things of which we should make the best we can but which is
ultimately indifferent to us. It is certainly of no importance to the
Epicurean universe as a whole how you behave, and moral virtue,
as we have seen, is justified only as a means to the end of the
most pleasant life for you as an individual.

The question what part concern for other human beings plays,
both in Stoic and in Epicurean ethics, will concern us in Chapter
Six. First, though, it seems appropriate to turn to those for whom
human happiness was not based on any dogmatic theory, either
concerning the universe or concerning human nature.

THE SCEPTICS

The Pyrrhonian sceptics as represented by Sextus reported, as we
saw in Chapter Two, that they were led to suspension of judgement
about everything. This brought freedom from anxiety or disturbance – *ataraxia*, the same term as was used by the Epicureans –
because those who do not commit themselves to the view that
death or illness, say, are great evils will be less perturbed by them.
But this, characteristically, is reported as something which simply
happens:

Scepticism is a power that sets appearances and thoughts
against one another in whatever way it may be; from it,
on account of the equal strength in the opposed facts and
arguments, we come first of all to suspension of judgement
and after this to being free from anxiety.

(Sextus, *PH* 1.8)

The Pyrrhonian sceptic does not dogmatically assert freedom from anxiety or disturbance to be the good (though this is less certain where Pyrrho himself is concerned), even though the belief that it is so may be the original *starting* point of the inquiry:

> The originating cause of scepticism is, we say, the hope of coming to be free from anxiety. For people with great natural talent, who were made anxious by the inconsistency in things, and were at a loss as to which of them they should rather assent to, came to inquire what is true in things and what false, on the assumption that they would achieve a state free from anxiety by deciding these things. But the principle of the sceptical system is most of all that to every argument there is opposed an equal argument; for we seem as a result of this to end by ceasing to dogmatise.
>
> (Sextus, *PH* 1.12)

Once the Sceptic has arrived at suspension of judgement (though 'arrived' could mislead; as we have seen in Chapter Two, this is a provisional attitude in the context of ongoing inquiry, not a goal reached definitively once and for all) such freedom from anxiety will presumably seem to be a good, but not be dogmatically asserted as such. To those who denied that it was a good at all the Sceptics would, as Hankinson has recently pointed out, have nothing to say,[21] except to cast doubt on any *other* good they claimed to recognise.

The question, however, remains: how is the Sceptic to live his life without committing himself to any judgements? The answer is, through the fourfold guidance of nature, affections or emotions, customs and skills; he will do certain things because it is natural or customary to do so, but without any commitment:

> Attending to appearances, then, we live in accordance with the observances of life undogmatically, since we cannot be altogether inactive. This observance seems to have four parts, part of it consisting in the guidance of nature, part in the compulsion of the affections, part in the tradition of laws and customs, and part in instruction in skills. The guidance of nature is that according to which we are naturally capable of sensation and thought; the compulsion of the affections is that by which hunger leads us to food and thirst to drink; the tradition of customs and laws is that by which we

114

regard piety in life as good and impiety as base; instruction in skills is that by which we are not incapable of activity in the skills we take up. But we say all these things undogmatically.

(Sextus, *PH* 1.23–4)

6

WHAT ABOUT OTHER PEOPLE?

SELF-INTEREST AND SOCIETY

A common criticism of Hellenistic moral philosophy is that it is self-centred; the agent's concern is ultimately with his or her own self-interest, and altruistic behaviour therefore seems to be ruled out. As already indicated in the opening section of Chapter Five, we should beware of contrasting reprehensible selfishness and utter selflessness as the only two possibilities; enlightened self-interest may imply regard for other people. Indeed, failure to realise that selflessness and greed were not the only alternatives may have contributed to the tendency in the 1980s, once self-interest *was* admitted as respectable at all, to regard ruthless competition as the only basis on which human life – one can hardly call it 'society' in such a context – could be organised.

However that may be, both Epicureans and Stoics certainly were committed to the standard ancient Greek view that the goal of life was individual happiness, and it was in terms of their – very different – concepts of this that we need to understand their views on how one should behave towards other people.

THE EPICUREANS

Justice, for Epicurus, has no existence in its own right – it is based on a social contract, or, as he put it, 'the agreement not to harm or be harmed' (*PD* 33 = LS 22A). But this does not mean that what is just and what is not is simply a matter of what agreements a particular society reaches. The existence of *some* agreement is a natural part of the development of human societies (Lucretius, 5.1019ff. = LS 22K; significantly, the point is put in terms of forming *friendships*; see pp. 118–20), and a particular agreement is only just if it benefits the members of the society who made it. If the circumstances of a society change, an agreement that was previously just can cease to be so, even if it is still agreed upon. Justice applies only to humans capable of making actual contracts, not to animals who cannot make contracts nor yet to human peoples who have been unable or unwilling to do so (Epicurus, *PD* 32 = LS 22A). But contracts can be broken; some individuals fail to realise that it is in their best interest to abide by the agreement neither to do nor suffer harm; it is at this point that legal sanctions become necessary,[1] and that political structures to enforce them have value.[2]

Legal sanctions, however, are one thing, the motivation of individuals another. Even if justice exists because it is to the advantage of the majority of people, why should an individual not go against it if he or she can be sure of getting away with doing so – especially if the pursuit of pleasure is the overriding consideration in life? True, the Epicurean view of how a pleasant life can be obtained is hardly one that would encourage the sort of self-indulgence that might need criminal behaviour to provide its resources. But more than that, Epicurus argued that the desire for freedom from anxiety should itself deter people from committing crimes; no one who commits a crime can be sure that he will not be found out – many criminals have given themselves away by talking in their sleep, as Lucretius notes (5.1156ff. = LS 22L) – and the inevitable anxiety that results from criminal behaviour simply, it is alleged, makes the crime not worth it in the first place:

> Injustice is not an evil in itself, but in the fear relating to the apprehension that one will not escape the notice of those appointed to punish such things.
>
> It is not possible, for the person who does anything in secret contravention of the agreement people [have made] with one another with a view to neither inflicting nor suffering harm, to be confident of escaping notice, even if this happens countless times for the moment; for until one's death it is not clear that one will also *continue* to escape notice.
>
> (*PD* 34–5 = LS 22A)

To some critics this has seemed an impossibly feeble justification for moral behaviour; to others, such as Victor Goldschmidt,[3] the Epicurean theory of law and justice has seemed more strongly

117

founded just because it is based on natural human instincts rather than on metaphysical dogmas concerning the divine government of the universe. And, as Annas (299–302) and others have stressed, we misunderstand Epicurus' theory if we interpret it in the light of a negative conception of human nature and of the social contract as a reluctant second-best (as in Plato, *Republic* 2 358E–359A, where the theory set up for Socrates to attack describes people as agreeing not to harm others only because they lack confidence in their own ability to prevail in a free-for-all; cf. LS p. 135). For Epicurus to live justly is not a second-best but, positively, a pleasant way to live.

The Epicurean will not, however, be much involved in the affairs of society. He will rather – at least in Epicurus' original conception – withdraw from public life to live with a community of Epicurean friends, as Epicurus himself did in the Garden:[4]

> Security from people, which is brought about up to a point by a certain power to drive away [what threatens us], is achieved in the most abundant and unmixed way in the security which comes from quietness and withdrawal from the affairs of the majority.
>
> *(PD 14)*

This, however, raises another problem: how can friendship be so important for the Epicurean if his ultimate concern is with his own pleasure? After all, friendship and commitment to others brings the risk of one's own tranquillity being disturbed, either through the efforts one must make on behalf of a friend or through anxiety at his or her misfortunes.

Admittedly, if the Epicurean need not be greatly troubled about misfortune, pain or death that may occur to himself, he need not be concerned about those that may occur to a friend either; and the benefits of friendship outweigh the disadvantages. These benefits were certainly stressed:

> Of the things which wisdom provides with a view to blessedness in the whole of life, much the greatest is the acquisition of friendship.
>
> *(PD 27 = LS 22E)*

Friendship dances round the inhabited world proclaiming to

all of us that we should wake up to congratulate one another
on our blessedness.

(Epicurus, *Vatican Sayings* 52 = LS 22F)

One may indeed suspect that part of the advantage of the Epicurean community for its members was that being with those of
like mind helped to ward off any intellectual doubts, a phenom-
enon not unknown with more recent sects.

But can a friendship entered into purely for the sake of the
benefits it brings really be called friendship? Aristotle had
expressly distinguished friendship based on mutual advantage,
friendship based on pleasure and the true friendship for its own
sake of the wise (*EN* 8.3); but for Epicureans, for whom pleasure
is the universal goal, this distinction does not seem to be available.

Some interpreters, notably Phillip Mitsis, have suggested that
pleasure turns out not after all to be the single goal of life for
Epicurus, and that friendship had independent and non-derivative
value. This, however, seems at odds with the whole structure of
his system. There is indeed a saying of Epicurus that 'All friendship
is worthy of choice [or: a virtue][5] on its own account, but it takes
its origin from mutual benefit' (Epicurus, *Vatican Sayings* 23 = LS
22F). But this need not be understood as implying that friendship
is to be pursued for some reason other than pleasure – the point is
rather that it is worthy of choice because of the pleasure it brings
in itself, and not only because it secures pleasure indirectly, as a
means to an end (by providing security, for instance). Cicero, *On
Ends* 1.66–70 (= LS 22O) reports three views held in the Epicurean
school, one which stresses the mutual benefits of friendship, a
second, that of 'certain Epicureans more timid in face of [Aca-
demic] criticisms', which holds that friendship based on mutual
advantage develops into a type where this ceases to be a necessary
ingredient, and a third which holds that the wise love each other
no less than themselves and that this in itself brings pleasure. The
second of these views can be understood in terms of pleasure as
the sole good (*contra* LS p. 138) if the claim that friends come to
be loved for their own sake rather than for advantage is interpreted
simply as asserting that friendship ceases to be purely an *instrumental* good and becomes pleasant in itself.

Even so, it seems difficult to explain the assertion that a wise
person will sometimes even be prepared to die for a friend,
attributed to Epicurus by DL 10.120 = LS 22Q, in terms of the

pursuit of one's own pleasure. Death is not in itself painful or to be regretted, but dying for a friend could hardly be justified in Epicurean terms unless one were to argue that doing so is a supremely pleasant act, that is to say that it makes a supreme contribution to achieving a life with the least pain and anxiety. Perhaps dying for a friend could be justified on the grounds that the sort of friendship that is needed for mutual support would simply not be possible unless people felt that their friends were committed enough to die for them. Epicurus points out that we need, not so much assistance itself, as the confidence that it will be there when needed (*Vatican Sayings* 34 = LS22F). One might on occasion fail to carry the commitment through when the crunch came; but – it might be argued – if people reneged on such commitments consistently and calculatingly, true friendship would soon disappear altogether. Another possibility might be that, as in the case of justice, remorse at the thought that one failed to die for a friend when one had a duty to do so would exclude living a pleasant life subsequently; but that just raises the question why one should, in Epicurean terms, think one had such a duty.

Leaving aside the question of why one should *die* for a friend, the troubles and effort commitment to a friend may more generally involve might be justified in terms of the long-term pleasure that the existence of a friendship will bring. Epicurus tells us explicitly that we should run risks for the sake of friendship (*Vatican Sayings* 28 = LS 22F); and the claim of his philosophy is not, after all, that we should run no risks at all – there is no reason to think that it is possible for a human being to escape *all* risks – but that we should minimise risks as far as possible. Even so, the critic may object that this is not real friendship: the friend's good is secondary, one's own pleasure is the ultimate aim. And, as Annas has pointed out, Epicurus cannot answer this by drawing a distinction between concern for the interests of others as a motive on a particular occasion, on the one hand, and a general aim directed towards the pleasure the continued friendship will bring, on the other; for '*every action* must be referred to nature's end' (*PD* 25 = LS 21E; my emphasis). This does not mean that a present pain may not be accepted for the sake of a long-term pleasure – that is a basic part of Epicurean ethics; but it does mean that a present action cannot be detached from the motive of pleasure altogether and interpreted entirely in terms of concern for others.

A further problem concerns the relation of the Epicurean, not just to his or her friends, but to the rest of society. The Epicurean community can all too easily appear as parasitic – taking advantage of the reasonable degree of order in society at large (protection of private property, for instance) which others take steps to preserve, but making no contribution itself to the general good. Cicero opens his *Republic* (*De Re Publica*) with a prolonged attack (1.1–11) on those who reject involvement in politics, and are clearly to be identified with the Epicureans, even though in the present fragmentary state of the text they are not actually named.

Indeed the attitude of the Epicurean to the outsider may appear callous:

> Sweet is it, when the winds stir up the waters on the vast sea, to watch from land the great struggling of another; not because there is pleasure and joy in anyone's trouble, but because it is sweet to see what troubles you yourself are free from. Sweet too is it to see great contests of war arranged across the field of battle when you do not share in the danger. But nothing is more delightful than to occupy the lofty sanctuaries of the wise, well fortified by the calm of learning, from which you can look down on others and see them go astray everywhere and, wandering, seek a path through life, competing with their talents, striving for status, struggling night and day with outstanding effort to rise up to the summit of power and gain control of affairs. Wretched minds of mortals, blind hearts! In what darkness and danger is this short period of life spent . . . [6]
>
> (Lucretius, 2.1–16 = LS 21W)

However, as Lucretius makes clear, his intention is not to gloat, but rather to recognise the blessings that Epicureanism brings and from which others in their folly exclude themselves. From the Epicurean point of view the problem is the reverse: why should Epicureans be concerned about non-Epicureans, and why should they seek to persuade them to their way of thinking? Why, in particular, did Epicurus and Lucretius take the trouble to leave writings calculated to do this? It would have been no loss to Epicurus himself if his creed had eventually been forgotten. One might argue that, whatever actually happened eventually, the belief that it would survive would be more pleasant for Epicurus during his own life than the reverse would have been. But then why *should* it matter to him that others should accept his views, whether in his own lifetime or subsequently? And how, in Epicurean terms, can Diogenes of Oenoanda's massive and expensive attempt to persuade his fellow-citizens be justified? Not, presumably, because of the good of those others, ultimately (even though Diogenes claims, questionably in Epicurean terms, that future generations 'belong to us, even if they have not yet been born'; p. 133); the reason for persuading others must be in terms of one's own happiness.

It might be suggested that the Epicurean will be more secure if society as a whole adopts Epicurean values. There is indeed a section of Diogenes' inscription which seems to speak of an eventual 'Epicurean millennium' when the institutions of non-Epicurean society will have withered away:

> Then in very truth the life of the gods will be transferred to human beings. All will be filled with justice and mutual friendship, and there will be no need for ramparts or laws and all the things we contrive on account of one another.
> (Diogenes of Oenoanda fr. 56 Smith = LS 22S)

But it is not clear whether Diogenes is representing Epicurus' own thoughts accurately here (cf. LS vol. 2, p. 143), and in any case it hardly seems likely that, in Epicurus' or Diogenes' own lifetimes (which is all that should, by their own principles, concern them), enough people could be won over to Epicurean ways of thinking to make a real difference to the Epicureans' security.

Perhaps, then, the answer might lie rather in the idea that there is a pleasure for oneself in doing good to others (and, for an Epicurean, persuading someone else of the truth of Epicureanism is probably the greatest good you can do to them). There is no intrinsic inconsistency between the notion that one may do good to others because it is pleasant to do so, and the principle that one's own pleasure is the ultimate goal, in themselves; a problem would arise only if one did good to others even when, pleasurable though it might be, it was not in fact the way to achieve the most pleasant life for oneself. That problem certainly arises, as we have seen, in the case of dying for a friend; it may raise questions about whether Epicurean friendship can, consistently with Epicurus' own principles, be friendship as others would understand the term. But there does not seem to be any inconsistency in arguing that a certain degree of other-regarding behaviour may on occasion be one pleasure among others and sometimes one that it is right to choose. Indeed Plutarch (*One Cannot Live a Pleasant Life by*

Following Epicurus 1097A = LS 22G) cites it as an Epicurean view that it is more pleasant to give a benefit than to receive one. Lucretius, however – constrained indeed by the requirements of a literary dedication – speaks not of pleasure in doing good, but of pleasure in the hoped-for *friendship* of Memmius:

> But your excellence and the hoped-for pleasure of sweet friendship urge me to endure every effort, and lead me to stay awake through the tranquil nights, trying to find with what poetic utterances I can set clear lights before your mind, lights by which you will be able to see deep into hidden things.
>
> (Lucretius, 1.140–5)

THE STOICS

For the Stoics relationships with other people form a central part of the doctrine of *oikeiôsis* or 'appropriation'; it is natural for us to be concerned for other human beings (Cicero, *On Ends* 3.62ff. = LS 57F). Hierocles in c. AD 100 indicated how we should progressively draw those in the outer circles of our concern towards the centre (Stobaeus, *Selections* 4.27.23, p. 671.7ff. Wachsmuth–Hense = LS 57G), though it can be objected (Annas 268) – much as Aristotle (*Politics* 2.3) objected to Plato's transformation of the Guardians in the *Republic* into a single happy quasi-family – that this would in practice just lead to a dilution of affection.

Social *oikeiôsis* and *oikeiôsis* to oneself, discussed in Chapter Five, develop together, as Annas stresses (275–6); it is not that the social aspect is a secondary and dependent one. But that does not alter the fact that the ultimate motivation for virtuous behaviour in Stoicism is concern for one's own virtue. The Stoic sage who helps someone else is not in the end concerned with whether the outcome for the other person is successful or not; but then he or she is not concerned with the actual outcome for himself or herself either. And, whatever the motive, the practical effect will be the same: the sage will attempt to treat other people in a way that is in accordance with natural affinity as the Stoics understand it. The Stoic will not refrain from helping others when it is the right thing to do, or fail to do what justice demands.

However, as with the Epicurean, so with the Stoic one may indeed ask whether true friendship is possible between people whose ultimate concern is not for each other but, in this case, for their own virtue. The Stoics found themselves having to answer the moral conundrum, originated by the Academic sceptic Carneades: if two shipwrecked sailors find themselves clinging to a plank that will only support one, what should they do? The answer of Panaetius' pupil Hecaton, reported by Cicero, *On Duties* 3.90, is that the one whose existence is more important, for himself or for other people, should stay on the plank, the other let go; if there is nothing to choose between them, they should draw lots. The introduction of randomness may seem absurd; but what is important is not to survive but to act rightly, and the absurdity of randomness avoids the arguably greater absurdity of its being appropriate for both men to fight to stay on the plank, or alternatively of its being appropriate for both of them to jump off so that neither survives.[7]

The Stoic duty to treat others justly still leaves open, however, the question how much involvement in political and public affairs is actually right. The early Stoa seems to have left that question open, to depend on the circumstances in each case (Stobaeus, *Selections* 2.7.11m, p. 109.15 Wachsmuth–Hense = LS 67W), though Seneca can draw a neat contrast between Epicurus, who says that 'the wise person will not engage in politics, unless some special circumstance disturbs him', and Zeno the Stoic, who says that the wise person 'will engage in politics unless something prevents it' (Seneca, *On Leisure*, 3.2). Subsequently, in the Roman period, Stoicism came to be contrasted with Epicureanism, as a philosophy of practical involvement; but it was also linked with republican opposition to the emperors, and aroused hostility and persecution just because it was seen as a principled, and therefore dangerous, opting out of the present state of society. As Miriam Griffin has shown, the objection to Stoicism from an emperor's point of view was that it provided an alternative authority, that of reason.[8]

Stoic political thought takes up themes from the Cynics, themes that can indeed be traced back even further, to the fifth century BC: the questioning of the laws and customs of existing states, and a stress on the natural as opposed to the conventional. Zeno, while still a pupil of the Cynic Crates (DL 7.4), wrote a *Republic* which shared some features (such as community of wives) with Plato's (DL 7.32–3 = LS 67B) but differed from it in that Plato described an ideal city ruled by the wise for the benefit of all its inhabitants, while Zeno described a city containing *only* the wise.[9]

124

This later came to be interpreted in terms of a world-wide community of the wise. Plutarch portrays Alexander the Great as putting into practice what for Zeno was only theory:

> Indeed the greatly admired *Republic* of Zeno, who founded the Stoic school, has this one thing as its aim, in short, that we should not live in cities or villages, each group distinguished by its own private [system of] justice, but should consider all people our fellow-villagers and fellow-citizens, and there should be a single way of life and order, as of a herd pastured together and nourished by a common law. Well, Zeno wrote this having fashioned a dream or image of a philosopher's republic [constitution, *politeia*] well-ordered by law, but Alexander turned word into deed.
>
> (Plutarch, *On the Fortune of Alexander the Great* 329AB = LS 67A)

This, however, seems to be the hindsight of a later period; Plutarch certainly disregards the fact that Zeno's ideal state was confined to the wise. Malcolm Schofield has suggested that Zeno may have said that the city of the wise was based on common, i.e. true and natural, law, and Plutarch wrongly took this to mean it was a *universal* city.[10] The connection of human with divine law is yet another point the Stoics derived from the Presocratic Heraclitus, who said that 'all human laws are nourished by one law, that which is divine' (KRS 250).

Chrysippus, whose own *Republic*, based on Zeno's, was notorious for saying that cannibalism could be acceptable (Sextus, *PH* 3.247–8 = LS 67G; the point presumably being that the prohibition against it is a cultural, not a natural, one), does seem to have regarded the world as a whole as a city in which the wise share fellow-citizenship. Schofield has suggested (op. cit. 70ff.) that the foundation of this idea is that all the wise will follow the same law, that of reason, and will hold the same views concerning society, so that on this basis they can be described as the citizens of a single state. Indeed any act of a sage will benefit every other sage (Plutarch, *CN* 1068F).[11] Diogenes the Cynic had claimed to be a citizen of the universe, in the negative sense of rejecting the arbitrary arrangements of individual states;[12] Aristo shared with the fifth-century BC sophist Hippias (Plato, *Protagoras* 337C) the idea that distinctions of nationality are unnatural (Plutarch, *On Exile* 600E = LS 67H), and Chrysippus held, with the typical Stoic

love of paradox, that ordinary cities are not real cities since they
are not morally good (Clement, *Miscellanies* 4.26 172.2; Annas
304), though not in practice rejecting normal civic life totally.

Nevertheless, Stoic political theory in this period has its limitations. With the rejection of cities in the ordinary sense goes, as
Annas (306–7) complains, a lack of interest in specific political
structures; the Stoics are interested in how to behave morally in
public life rather than with political reforms as such. One area
in which the Stoics have been subject to particular criticism is that
of slavery, a standard institution in ancient society which few
questioned altogether.[13] Aristotle had attempted to deal with it by
distinguishing between those who were naturally fitted to be
slaves, being incapable of organising their own lives, and those
who happened actually to be slaves, for example through defeat
in war; natural slaves existed, but those who were actually slaves
were not always those who ought to be (*Politics* 1.4–6). The Stoics,
on the other hand, concerned themselves not with developing a
theory or a critique of the institution of slavery, but with arguing
that the status of slave or free person was irrelevant to the true
freedom which the wise alone possess, whatever their actual circumstances; even a slave can be virtuous. The wise person alone
is free (see Chapter Four), and will be even if a slave; the wise
person is also (regardless of actual status) a king, as well as a
magistrate, a judge and an orator (DL 7.122 = LS 67M). Once
again, this invites Horace's ridicule:

> 'If the person who is wise is wealthy, and a good cobbler,
> and the only person who is handsome, and a king, why do
> you want what you already have?' 'You don't know', he
> says, 'what father Chrysippus says; the wise person has never
> made shoes or sandals for himself, and yet he is a cobbler.'
> 'How so?' 'Just as, although Hermogenes be silent, he is a
> singer and an excellent musician, and the crafty Alfenus, even
> when he threw away every tool of his trade and shut up
> shop, was a barber,[14] so the wise person alone is the best
> practitioner of every trade, and thus a king.' Playful children
> are pulling your philosophical beard . . .
>
> (Horace, *Satires* 1.3.124ff.)

But we are used by now to Stoic paradoxes.

Bernard Williams attacks the Stoic acceptance of slavery, describ-
ing the teaching that the slave's mind is free, even if his or her

body is not, as repulsive.[15] The Stoics do not, however, simply accept injustice in the social world because they regard the inner self as more important; rather, as we have seen in Chapter Three, they argue – rightly or wrongly – that everything that happens in the external world, including the enslavement of some rather than others, is the result of divine providence. Escapism is a charge that may be levelled with more justice not against Stoicism but against the Platonic tradition, which has characteristically (whatever Plato's own intentions) looked to a world better than this imperfect one. And as for slavery, some may find more to object to in Aristotle's justification of it – also attacked by Williams – by the argument that some people are naturally suited to be slaves, even if the classes of those fitted to be slaves and those who actually are slaves do not in practice coincide.

The notion of a shared world citizenship, not now confined to the wise, came to be allied, especially in the writings of Cicero, with the indigenous Roman doctrine of the 'law of nations'. That term applied to laws at Rome itself applying to non-citizens as well as to citizens; but it was also used in the wider senses of natural law, as opposed to the laws of specific states, and of 'international law' governing relations between states. The connection with Stoic ideas was a natural one; the Stoics had emphasised the importance of law, even if in the cosmic rather than the political sense, and the Stoic doctrine of the *oikeiôsis* of all human beings to one another provided a natural basis for a doctrine of natural law transcending political boundaries (Cicero, *Republic* 3.33 = LS 67S). A theme particularly developed in Cicero's writings is that of the universe as the common home of gods and human beings:

> First of all the world itself was made for the sake of gods and humans, and whatever there is in it was prepared and devised for the enjoyment of humans. For the world is, as it were, a common home of gods and humans, or the city of both groups; for only those who have the use of reason live by law and right.
>
> (Cicero, *On the Nature of the Gods* 2.154)

And, through the writings of Cicero, Stoic ideas were to play a significant part in the development of doctrines of natural law in Christian thought (notably in Augustine) and in the writings of jurists of the Renaissance and later.[16]

7

EPILOGUE

Three individuals may conclude our survey and draw some threads together. Two are Stoics: Epictetus the former slave and Marcus Aurelius the Roman emperor. Epictetus, as we have seen, lays particular emphasis on the distinction between what is in our power and what is not. The Hellenistic philosophy of the last three centuries BC has been interpreted as an individualistic reaction to the decline of the city-state; concentration on the individual, and emphasis on the individual's limitations, are even more apparent in Epictetus.

The question how important physics was to Stoic ethics in the Hellenistic period was discussed at the end of Chapter Five. In the Stoicism of the Roman Empire we find less concern with physics in general, though Seneca wrote eight books of *Questions* on natural science, with some moralising content. More typical of the period, however, is an emphasis not on the physical structure of the cosmos but on the divine spirit in each individual. The idea of such a spirit is already present in Chrysippus (DL 7.88), and the idea that the reason within us is part of the universal reason is standard in Stoicism from the beginning.[1] Posidonius, too, contrasted the divine spirit within us with the lowest part of the Platonically divided soul, and described the former as akin to the spirit that rules the world:

> The cause of the passions, that is, of discord and of an unhappy life, is failing to follow in everything the spirit (*daimôn*) within oneself, which is akin to and has the same nature as the spirit that manages the whole world, but [rather] falling away and being carried along with the inferior and animal-like spirit .... it is of primary importance in no

way to be led by the irrational and unhappy and godless aspect of the soul.

> (Posidonius cited by Galen, *PHP* 5.6.4–5 = Posidonius F187 EK)

But Epictetus uses the image far more directly:

> You are of primary importance, you are a portion of God; you have some part of him in yourself. Why then do you not recognise your kinship? Why do you not know whence you have come? Are you not willing to bear in mind, when you eat, who you are that is eating and whom you are nourishing? When you associate with people, who you are that is associating? When you are someone's companion, when you exercise, when you converse, do you not know that it is God you are nourishing, God you are exercising? You carry God round with you, wretch, and you do not know it.
>
> (Epictetus, *Discourses* 2.8.11)

> So, when you shut your doors and make darkness within, remember never to say that you are alone; you are not, but God is within and so is your guardian spirit (*daimôn*). And what need do these have of light to see what you are doing?
>
> (ibid., 1.14.13–14)

Seneca too has the idea of a divine spirit within us, and couples it with that of the virtuous person rising above fortune:

> A holy spirit dwells within us, the observer and guardian of our good and bad deeds. He treats us in the way he is treated by us. No human being is good without God; can anyone rise above fortune unless aided by him? He gives splendid and upright counsels. In every good person 'what god it is is uncertain, but a god dwells there'.[2]
>
> (Seneca, *Letters on Morals* 41.2)

The image is rather different from that of the dog in Chapter Four tied to and following the wagon. Indeed, as we saw in the quotation at the start of Chapter One, Horace applied the description 'rising above circumstances' not to Stoicism but to the Aristippean hedonism he contrasted with it.

It is, however, in Marcus Aurelius, more than any earlier Stoic, that we find a contrast between the world of our experience and a superior region. Traditional Stoic themes of universal nature and the kinship of the human race are combined with a playing down of the importance of the here and now:

> When you are annoyed at something, you have forgotten that everything comes about in accordance with the nature of the whole; and that the error was not yours; and in addition to this that everything that happens always happened in this way and will happen and now happens everywhere; and how great is the kinship of a human being with the whole human race, for it is sharing not in a little blood or a little seed but in intellect. You have also forgotten that each person's mind is a god, and has flowed from There; and that nothing is private to anyone, but the little child, and the little body, and the little soul itself have come from There; and that everything is supposition; and that each person lives only in the present and at once loses that.
>
> (Marcus Aurelius, *Meditations* 12.26)

('There', *ekei*, was a traditional, originally euphemistic, expression for the underworld; in Neoplatonism it would come to indicate the incorporeal Platonic Forms by contrast with what is bodily, apprehensible by the senses and subject to change.) Marcus sometimes sounds not unlike Plato in certain of his moods, and with hindsight his view of human experience can be seen as pointing to the replacement of Stoicism by Platonism as the dominant philosophy of late antiquity:

> Empty seriousness of a show, plays upon the stage, flocks, herds, battles with spears, a bone thrown to dogs, a morsel to the fish that receive it; strugglings of ants to bear their burdens, the travels of fluttering blowflies, puppets pulled by strings. Among these one must take one's stand graciously and without snorting insolently; but one should take note that each person is worth just as much as the things he or she takes seriously.
>
> (ibid., 7.3)

with which one may, following Rist,[3] compare from Plato himself:

> Human affairs, then, are not deserving of much serious concern; but it is necessary to be concerned, and this is not fortunate ... I say that it is necessary to be seriously con-

cerned about what is serious, but not about what is not; and that by nature God is deserving of all blessed concern, but human beings, as I said before, are contrived as a sort of plaything of God, and in reality this is the best thing about them.

(Plato, *Laws* 7 803bc)

Not that such ideas started with Plato; the idea that human activities provide amusement for the gods is as old as Homer's *Iliad*. The difference is that for Plato, and later for the Neoplatonists, immortality and rationality can give human beings a stake in the other, superior world. Marcus, however, is still a Stoic; he shares, indeed, the Stoic belief in a limited survival of the soul after the death of the body, but there is little emphasis on this, and an absence of the Platonic sense that human beings truly belong in another world or that there are rewards for virtue there. Cicero, named Father of his Country and by his own estimation greater than its founder Romulus (*Against Catiline* 3.2), presents rewards in heaven for great statesmen after death in his *Republic* as Scipio's dream. But in Marcus, ruler of the Roman Empire, even the dreams seem absent. For him we are very definitely part of the physical world and its processes:

Consider continually how many doctors have died, after often knitting their brows over their patients; how many astrologers, having foretold the deaths of others as if this were something important; how many philosophers, who contended endlessly about death or immortality; ... Go over how many people you have known, one after the other; one buried another and was then laid out for burial himself, and another another; all in a short time. In general, consider always how ephemeral and cheap human affairs are; yesterday slime,[4] tomorrow pickle[5] or ashes. Go through this momentary time in accordance with nature, and come to an end cheerfully, like an olive that falls when it is ripe, speaking well of earth who bore you and giving thanks to the tree that begat you.

(ibid., 4.48)

This draws, indeed, on traditional themes of consolation-literature, and identification of one's own interests with those of the world can also be a source of more positive-sounding inspiration:

Everything is in tune for me which is harmonious for you,
O world; nothing is premature or too late which is well
timed for you. For me everything which your seasons bring,
O nature, is a harvest: everything from you, everything in
you, everything directed towards you. The famous writer
said 'Dear City of Cecrops';[6] will you not say, 'Dear City of
God'?

(ibid., 4.23)

But the absence of other-worldly consolations makes the authenti-
cally Stoic tone of positive determination that emerges in Marcus'
writing all the more striking:

Of human life the duration is an instant; its substance is in
flux; its perception is faint; the whole composition of the
body is ready to decay; the soul is a child's toy; chance is
obscure; reputation is doubtful. In short everything to do
with the body is like a flowing river,[7] everything to do with
the soul a dream and a delusion. Life is a war and a sojourn
in a foreign country; subsequent reputation is oblivion. What
then is there that can escort one on one's way? *One thing
and one only, philosophy.* This consists in keeping the *daimôn*
within free from outrage and harm, superior to pleasures and
pains, doing nothing at random, not falsely or hypocritically,
not needing someone else to do anything or not to do it.
Also accepting what happens and is allotted, as coming from
some place from which one came oneself; and in all things
awaiting death with a cheerful mind, as being nothing other
than the dissolution of the elements from which each living
creature is composed. If for the elements themselves there is
nothing terrible in each continually being changed into
another, why should anyone look askance at the change and
dissolution of them all? It is in accordance with nature;
and *nothing evil is in accordance with nature.*

(ibid., 2.17; my emphasis)

And he can thus provide the summary in a single sentence of
Hellenistic philosophy as this book has attempted to present it:
'Just don't go on discussing what sort of person a good person
ought to be; be one' (ibid., 10.16).

132

* * *

Meanwhile passers-by at Oenoanda were reading Diogenes' still-recent inscription:

> But since, as I said before, the majority of people, as if in an epidemic, suffer a common sickness of false opinion about things, and their number is increasing (for in rivalry with one another one catches the disease from another, like sheep); and because it is right to assist those who will exist after us (for they too belong to us, even if they have not yet been born), and in addition it is an act of philanthropy to come to the aid of visiting foreigners – since the assistance from what I write reaches more people in this way, I chose to make use of this porch [Greek: *stoa!*] to set forth in public the saving remedies, remedies of which we ourselves have experience in every way. For we have been set free from the empty fears that held us in their grip, and of pains we have excised the empty ones altogether, and compressed the natural ones into a very small compass . . .
>
> (Diogenes of Oenoanda, fr. 3.IV–VI Smith)

NOTES

1 HELLENISTIC PHILOSOPHY: AIMS, CONTEXT, PERSONALITIES, SOURCES

1 Cf. Benson Mates, *Stoic Logic*, 2nd edn, Berkeley, University of California Press, 1961, 86–94.
2 Cf. especially two volumes in the Sather Classical Lectures series, separated by twenty-two years: Hugh Lloyd-Jones, *The Justice of Zeus*, Berkeley, University of California Press, 1971, 164, and Bernard Williams, *Shame and Necessity*, Berkeley, University of California Press, 1993, especially 8ff., 166f.
3 Admiral J. H. Stockdale, cited in *Epictetus: The Discourses, the Handbook, fragments*, ed. C. Gill, translation revised by R. Hard, London, Everyman (J. M. Dent), 1995, 347–9.
4 For a fuller account see D. N. Sedley, 'The Protagonists', in M. Schofield *et al.* (eds), *Doubt and Dogmatism*, Oxford, Clarendon Press, 1980, 1–19.
5 Cf. D. N. Sedley, 'Epicurus and his Professional Rivals', in J. Bollack and A. Laks (eds), *Études sur l'épicurisme antique*, Lille, Publications de l'Université de Lille III, 1976 (Cahiers de Philologie 1), 127–32.
6 Arnaldo Momigliano, *Journal of Roman Studies* 31 (1941), 149–57, especially 155–7, argued that it was indeed *conversion* to Epicureanism that prompted Cassius' action, but this has been questioned by more recent writers. Cicero, *Republic* 1.10, attributes to opponents of political involvement – Epicureans, though not explicitly identified as such – the exception that the wise person will take part in public affairs if compelled to do so in a crisis. See Chapter Six, and on Epicureanism at Rome in the first century BC see also M. Griffin in M. Griffin and J. Barnes, eds, *Philosophia Togata*, Oxford, Clarendon Press, 1989, 1–37; Howard Jones, *The Epicurean Tradition*, London, Routledge, 1989, 75–6; J. G. F. Powell, ed., *Cicero the Philosopher*, Oxford, Clarendon Press, 1995, 28–9.
7 Martin Ferguson Smith, *Diogenes of Oenoanda: the Epicurean Inscription*, Naples, Bibliopolis, 1993, 86–7 and 92.

2 HOW DO WE KNOW ANYTHING?

1 Aristotle, *Rhetoric* 1. 1355a14: 'it belongs to the same capacity to see the truth and what is like the truth, and human beings have an adequate natural capacity for the truth and for the most part achieve truth.' See also Aristotle, *Metaphysics* α. 1 993a30–b9.

2 *EN* 1.8 1098b27, 10.2 1172b36.

3 LS pp. 85–6 compare the camera, which cannot lie, because it represents accurately the image of the object as seen by the camera, and yet takes photographs of objects rather than of images of objects.

4 On this see I. G. Kidd, 'Theophrastus' *Meteorology*, Aristotle and Posidonius', in W. W. Fortenbaugh and D. Gutas (eds), *Theophrastus: His Psychological, Doxographical, and Scientific Writings*, New Brunswick, Transaction, 1992 (Rutgers University Studies in Classical Humanities, 5), 294–306.

5 LS pp. 96–7 question Sextus' (*M* 7.214 = LS 18A) citation of this as an example of contestation, pointing out that the weight of the argument rests not on the observation that motion exists, but rather on the argument, from the analogy with sensible things, that motion requires void. But *ad Hdt.* 51 seems to suggest that attestation, contestation, and the absence of the two between them cover *all* cases where inference from sense-perception leads to a true judgement; and sense-perception is for Epicurus the basis of all knowledge.

6 Cf. LS p. 32.

7 Centaurs are impossible because the horse part and the human part would age at different rates: Lucretius, 5.878ff.

8 'Aëtius' was the name given by Diels, on the evidence of a passage in Theodoret, to the author of a lost work which he reconstructed, arguably with a certain amount of forcing of the evidence, from texts in Stobaeus and pseudo-Plutarch. See KRS p. 5 for more details. I print the author's name between scare-quotes because some scholars have questioned the attribution of the text to an author of this name, and more have questioned the method of Diels' reconstruction. Nevertheless, it remains a convenient way of referring to Stobaeus and/or pseudo-Plutarch as printed in parallel columns at each point in Diels' edition.

9 No coalescing of external thought-images being required here, by contrast with the Epicurean theory.

10 As opposed to those resulting from teaching and deliberate thought ('Aëtius', loc. cit.). In another sense the development of these concepts too must be a part of nature, for everything that happens in the Stoic universe is in accordance with the nature of that universe as a whole; more on this in Chapter Three.

11 Thus David Glidden (in Stephen Everson (ed.), *Language* (Companions to Ancient Thought, 3), Cambridge, Cambridge University Press, 1994, 135) has suggested that we should call the Stoics 'nativists' rather than 'empiricists'. In saying that something just and good is conceived of naturally the text in Diogenes Laertius is not denying that other concepts too arise naturally – indeed, as we have

seen, all preconceptions do so; 'naturally' in this case is simply standing in for the full and complex account of how this particular concept develops.

12 Cf. LS pp. 258–9 on the question whether assent to an apprehensive impression by someone other than a sage counts as opinion or not; one passage (Stobaeus *Selections* 2.7.11m, p. 111.2–5 Wachsmuth–Hense = LS 41G) suggests this. The term 'sage' is archaic and may have misleading connotations of *ancient* wisdom; I use it partly because it is gender-neutral and 'wise person' seems cumbrous. Both women and men can be philosophers for the Stoics: Lactantius, *Divine Institutes* 3.25 = *SVF* 3.253; Musonius Rufus, fr. 3 (= Stobaeus, *Selections* 2.31.126, pp. 244.6–246.2 Wachsmuth–Hense; translated by C. E. Lutz in *Yale Classical Studies* 10 (1947), 38–43; cf. Nussbaum 322–4). The archaic 'sage' may also serve as a reminder that for the Stoics the wise person is as rare as the phoenix (Chapter Five), though the Stoics themselves do not use an out-of-the-ordinary term to make this point: to do so would be contrary to their customary liking for pointing up paradoxes rather than defusing them.

13 M. Frede in Stephen Everson (ed.), *Language* (Companions to Ancient Thought, 3), Cambridge, Cambridge University Press, 1994, 118ff.

14 Or, since it amounts to saying 'if p then q' ≡ 'not both [p and not-q]', of the Boolean algebra on which, among other things, electronic computing is ultimately based, for logical conjunction ['and'] and disjunction ['or'] can be represented as algebraic products and sums respectively; if 1 = true and 0 = false, 'a and b' can be represented by a multiplied by b, which is 1 only if a and b both are.

15 Cf. on these arguments W. and M. Kneale, *The Development of Logic*, Oxford, Clarendon Press, 1962, 172–4.

16 Cf. Benson Mates, *Stoic Logic*, 2nd edn, Berkeley, University of California Press, 1961, 76.

17 Cf. Michael Frede in Myles Burnyeat (ed.), *The Skeptical Tradition*, Berkeley, University of California Press, 1983, 89ff.; LS pp. 251–2.

18 Harold Tarrant, *Scepticism or Platonism?*, Cambridge, Cambridge University Press, 1985. R. J. Hankinson, *The Sceptics*, London, Routledge, 1995, 119 suggests that Philo's claim that things are knowable in their own natures may rather mean that we can have knowledge without realising that we do.

19 Cf. Hankinson, op. cit., 26, 302. Where Pyrrho is concerned, Marcel Conche has argued (*Pyrrhon ou l'apparence*, Paris, Presses Universitaires de France, 1994) that talk of an external reality is for him altogether out of place, and that where Sextus will speak of the Sceptic as searching and as *suspending* judgement, Pyrrho rejected the whole idea of making any judgements about the external world at all. It is true that some of the reports, such as Timon's 'that honey is sweet I do not assert, but that it seems so I do agree' (DL 9.105 = LS 1H), do seem to contrast appearance and reality; however, it is impossible explicitly to reject talk of an external reality without mentioning it in doing so.

20 The Pyrrhonist, unlike the Academic sceptic, does not rule out the

possibility that an apprehensive presentation might turn up one day: Hankinson, op. cit., 114–15.

21 Cf. LS pp. 16–18; Richard Bett, 'Aristocles on Timon on Pyrrho', *Oxford Studies in Ancient Philosophy* 12 (1994), 137–81.

22 On the other hand Cicero, *Academica* 1.45 = LS 68A attributes to Arcesilaus the denial that we can know even the one thing Socrates claimed to know, that he knew nothing.

23 Hankinson, op. cit., 135, of Aenesidemus.

24 Hankinson, op. cit., 300.

25 Ibid., 298ff.; he explains the apparent conflict between this and passages that speak of weighing up arguments (*PH* 1.26, 196, 202–6; Hankinson, op cit., 300) by the relativisation of sceptical reports to their therapeutic context, on which see further on p. 32.

26 M.F. Burnyeat, 'Can the Sceptic Live his Scepticism?', in M. Schofield *et al.* (eds), *Doubt and Dogmatism*, Oxford, Clarendon Press, 1980, 49ff.

27 Hankinson, op. cit., 297ff.

3 WHAT IS REALITY?

1 In an explicitly cosmic context in *Laws* X; the idea of soul as an epiphenomenon, produced by and supervening on the arrangement of the bodily constituents, had already been rejected in *Phaedo* 92–4.

2 Expressed by Lucretius in terms of 'laws of nature', *foedera naturai*, which result from the structure of matter – the fact that certain types of atoms fit together in certain ways rather than others – rather than being imposed on it by any separate power or being. Cf. Lucretius, 2.700ff.; A. A. Long, 'Chance and Natural Law in Epicureanism', *Phronesis* 22 (1977), 63–88.

3 Aristotle, *Physics* 2.4 196a24ff. = KRS 568, criticises unnamed philosophers who attribute the existence of the heavens to a chance vortex (*dinê*) – as Leucippus and Democritus did the origin of each world-system, cf. KRS 563, 566 – but assert regularity in the growth of animals and plants.

4 Lucretius' inclusion among his examples of the fact that birds do not suddenly appear in mid-air (1.162 = LS 4B) on the face of it blurs this distinction; however, air is not in fact empty space. The observation that things take time to grow and develop (1.184ff.) relates more to (A) than to (B); the point for Lucretius may indeed be that time is needed for seeds of the *right kind* to be found, but that is to assume in advance that the atomic theory, explaining properties of things through the shape of their 'seeds', is the correct one.

5 Aristotle indeed recognises that a saw, for instance, needs to be made of metal rather than (e.g.) wood (*Physics* 2.9 200a28). But what is present in the atomist theory, and not in his, is the belief that being of one type rather than another is an *inherent feature* of individual pieces of matter.

6 The *Letter to Herodotus* is, after all, explicitly written for those already

familiar with the system. On the relation between proof and exposition in Lucretius, and its bearing on the rhetorical rather than philosophical character of the poem, there is an illuminating discussion by C. J. Classen, 'Poetry and Rhetoric in Lucretius', *Transactions of the American Philological Association* 99 (1968), 77-118, reprinted (also in English) in C. J. Classen (ed.), *Probleme der Lukrezforschung*, Hildesheim, Olms, 1986, 331–74.

7 Or, in the case of Anaxagoras, *all* sensible stuffs. See A. P. D. Mourelatos, 'The Real, Appearances, and Human Error in Early Greek Philosophy', *Review of Metaphysics* 19 (1965), 346–65.

8 Because the total number of atoms of all shapes is infinite; and that must be so because space is infinite, and a finite number of atoms in infinite space would never come together and form compounds (*ad Hdt.* 42 = LS 10A; Lucretius, 1.1017ff.).

9 Bailey, in particular, argued that 'particles' in such contexts should be understood, though Lucretius was not himself clear on the point, to apply not to individual atoms but to clusters or 'nuclei' composed of them (C. Bailey (ed.), *Lucretius: De Rerum Natura*, Oxford, Clarendon Press, 1947, vol. 2, pp. 866, 1020, 1038–9). It is indeed, as Bailey argued, not the case, in the example at Lucretius, 2.391ff., that just one atom of a liquid goes through each hole in a strainer. But this need not imply that 'nuclei' have any permanence or any particular significance in the physical theory; in particular there is no suggestion that the 'nuclei' have the function that molecules do in the modern atomic theory, namely that several different types of atoms form combinations which *already at the molecular level* have clearly defined sets of properties characteristic of molecules of certain types and different from those of their constituent atoms.

10 Cf. *ad Hdt.* 41 = LS 10A, dramatised by Lucretius, 1.968ff. = LS 10B in the image of the man running up to the edge of the universe and throwing a javelin; will it fly onwards (in which case we weren't at the edge) or not (in which case we weren't at the edge either, because there must be something beyond to stop the javelin). A text attributed to the Aristotelian Alexander of Aphrodisias (c. AD 200), who *does* believe in a finite universe, attempts to answer this by saying that analogies from our terrestrial appearance need not apply at the edge of the universe: R. W. Sharples, *Alexander of Aphrodisias: Quaestiones 2.16–3.15*, London, Duckworth, 1994, 73.

11 This assumes, indeed, that there are indivisible minima not only of bodies but also of space. But the Aristotelian argument makes the same supposition, and in any case the argument could be recast in terms of the first atom moving in an eastwards direction past exactly one indivisible minimal part of a third atom.

12 It seems hard to suppose that the collisions and reboundings of the atoms cancel out the downward movement of everything entirely. One might indeed suppose that the collisions and reboundings are *superimposed* on the downwards fall, in such a way that we – being part of the downwards fall ourselves – would not be able to detect it at all. But Epicurus seems rather to have thought that atoms travelling

in any direction other than downwards tend, if left to themselves, to revert to the natural downwards direction; cf. the end of *ad Hdt.* 61 = LS 11E, an atom will move as quick as thought *'until* something impedes it, *either* from outside *or from its own weight* in relation to the force of what struck it' (my emphasis).

13 Epicurus nevertheless seems to have done so; *ad Hdt.* 60 asserts that a motion upwards above our heads will arrive countless times at the feet of those above us, but this is an assertion of the possibility of proceeding for ever in an upwards direction, not – as might at first be thought – an assertion that upwards and downwards are relative to an observer's position and different for different observers. The motion will arrive first at the *feet* of those above us; and this means that their 'up' and 'down' are the same as ours.

14 It has indeed been suggested that some atomist later than Democritus but before Epicurus held such a theory. This, however, seems questionable.

15 Since writing this, I have learned that a similar interpretation has been developed independently and in much more detail by Tim O'Keefe; see his forthcoming paper in *Phronesis* vol. 41 (1996) no. 3.

16 Cf. J. Worthington, *Wordsworth's Reading of Roman Prose*, New Haven, Yale University Press, 1946 (Yale Studies in English, 102) 52–3.

17 On the tensions introduced by Chrysippus' doctrine of *pneuma* cf. R. B. Todd, 'Monism and Immanence', in J. M. Rist (ed.), *The Stoics*, Berkeley, University of California Press, 1978, 153ff.

18 Cf. LS 47M–R. *Hexis* is the term translated by LS as 'tenor'.

19 Cf. LS p. 288.

20 I owe this analogy to Richard Sorabji.

21 Simplicius, *On Aristotle's* Categories 66.32 = LS 27F. 'Genera' is the ancient term; 'categories' has become customary modern usage, though the Stoic doctrine should be distinguished from Aristotle's doctrine of categories, which does not include the underlying indeterminate substrate as itself a category.

22 That fire feeds on moisture was a common ancient Greek belief; the ashes left by fire are dry, and the sun was often believed to be fuelled by the mists it draws up from water on the earth's surface. Living things require moisture; and living things are warm. Diogenes Laertius 7.136 = LS 46B indeed speaks of *Zeus* turning all substance into water; but presumably even the natural change which *extinguishes* the fire is due to the fire as active principle, since everything is.

23 This aspect has been particularly stressed by David E. Hahm, *The Origins of Stoic Cosmology*, Columbus, Ohio State University Press, 1977; see his ch. 5 for the treatment of the universe as a living being, and ch. 6, p. 194 for the idea of a life-cycle. The analogy is limited in one respect: for the universe, the conflagration is not seen in terms of death and destruction.

24 Notably by S. Sambursky, *Physics of the Stoics*, London, Routledge, 1959, 53–7.

25 I owe this suggestion to David Sedley.

26 J. M. Rist, *Stoic Philosophy*, Cambridge, Cambridge University Press, 1969, 217–18.

27 *Laws* 10 908E, cf. 899D.

28 Here I am following LS, pp. 145–9. The position is, however, complicated, and as has been seen some of the ancient evidence does give Epicurus' gods a separate existence in the *intermundia*. LS's discussion should be consulted.

4 WHAT ARE WE?

1 See Michael Frede, 'On Aristotle's Conception of the Soul', in M. C. Nussbaum and A. O. Rorty (eds), *Essays on Aristotle's* De Anima, Oxford, Clarendon Press, 1992, 93–107.

2 Lucretius, 3.854 = LS 24E. But where space as well as time is infinite the atoms that once formed a particular soul could wander infinitely far apart and never be reunited.

3 3.417–829; the exact number depends on how one divides the arguments up. Parts in LS 14FGH.

4 Some ancient Greek thinkers – notably Alcmaeon, Plato and Galen – located intelligence in the head; but this was a minority view. For Aristotle the brain functioned purely as a cooling device for the blood, somewhat like a car radiator.

5 Ironically enough, the discovery of the nervous system took place in the first half of the third century BC, very soon after Epicurus' own lifetime. (Cf. Julia Annas, *Hellenistic Philosophy of Mind*, Berkeley, University of California Press, 1992, 20–6.) But the Epicurean school was more interested in adopting a scientific stance for philosophical purposes than in keeping up to date with new scientific discoveries. See Chapter Two, on the Epicurean attitude to astronomical theories.

6 In the extant text of Epicurus, *ad Hdt.* 63 = LS 14A, only three, excluding Lucretius' air. But Lucretius' four ingredients are also found in a report of Epicurean doctrine in 'Aëtius' 4.3.11 = LS 14C, and a hot, a windy and an airy substance in Plutarch, *Against Colotes* 20.

7 D. J. Furley, *Two Studies in the Greek Atomists*, Princeton, Princeton University Press, 1967, part II.

8 Notably W. C. Englert, *Epicurus on the Swerve and Voluntary Action*, Atlanta, Scholars Press, 1987 (American Classical Studies, 16).

9 David Sedley, 'Epicurean anti-reductionism', in J. Barnes and M. Mignucci (eds), *Matter and Metaphysics*, Naples, Bibliopolis, 1989, 297–327.

10 See further R. W. Sharples, 'Mind and Matter: Epicurus and Carneades', *Bulletin of the Institute of Classical Studies* 38 (1991–3), 174–90. Strictly speaking, what would be involved may be not so much the correlation of choice and swerve – how does one identify a distinctive moment of choice anyway? – as the (more or less fuzzy) correlation of successive configurations of atoms and successive mental states; if the transition from one to another is not entirely determined in the case of the former, it need not be in that of the latter either.

11 Julia Annas has suggested (op. cit., 187) that the swerve and the fourth unnamed substance were *alternative* solutions to the problem of spontaneity.

12 A pattern repeated in the 'SWOT analysis' popular with business training consultants of the 1980s: 'strengths, weaknesses, opportunities, threats' relate to supposed goods and evils in the present (the first pair) and in the future (the second pair). The Stoics would endorse the emphasis here on reasoning positively about one's own possible courses of action, rather than being carried away by passions; they would reject any implication that a threat, for example, is an evil – it can at most be an unpreferred indifferent, and an opportunity for displaying virtue. They might not accept the criteria for a right decision in given circumstances that the advocates of the analysis would imply; and they would want to insist that setting out to achieve the right thing was more important than achieving it. See further in Chapter Five.

13 Cf. Stephen A. White in J. G. F. Powell (ed.), *Cicero the Philosopher*, Oxford, Clarendon Press, 1995, 244, citing Cicero, *Tusculan Disputations* 4.61.

14 I have assumed in the text that 'good feelings' relate to real good and evil, i.e. one's own virtue and wickedness, rather than to external circumstances, which, as we shall see in Chapter Five, are not truly good or evil but are nevertheless 'preferred' or 'unpreferred'. They are interpreted in the latter way by Nussbaum 399; in this case the point of 'wise avoidance' will rather be that, while an external threat cannot actually be evil, you should still try to avoid it if you can. But 'wish' and 'joy' should surely only have *real* good as their objects. I am grateful to Tad Brennan for enlightenment on these issues. There are sub-species of 'joy' and 'wish' that relate not to the sage's own virtue but to his joy in and wish for true good – i.e. virtue – in other sages. Cf. *SVF* 3.432 and Maximilian Forschner, *Die stoische Ethik*, Darmstadt, Wissenschaftliche Buchgesellschaft, 2nd edn, 1995, 139–40.

15 Brad Inwood, *Ethics and Human Action in Early Stoicism*, Oxford, Clarendon Press, 1985, 138–9.

16 Inwood, op. cit., 170–2, argues that Chrysippus' notion of an impulse which becomes excessive and escapes control is to be contrasted with the Platonic and Galenic notion of an element in the soul which is itself intrinsically irrational and will either be controlled by reason or escape its control.

17 Posidonius cited by Galen, *PHP* 4.3.2–5 = LS 65K.

18 Cf. K. J. Dover, *Greek Popular Morality*, Oxford, Blackwell, 1974, 116–129.

19 Cf. for the foregoing J. M. Rist, *Stoic Philosophy*, Cambridge, Cambridge University Press, 1969, 219–32, arguing forcefully that Seneca has not moved away from earlier Stoic intellectualism, and that his *voluntas* is the equivalent of Epictetus' *prohairesis*, 'choice' or 'policy', as the moral character of the individual as expressed in that individual's judgements. But Rist allows that Seneca's and indeed Epictetus' approach may have contributed to later belief in a faculty of will –

while insisting that this may not have been a helpful or desirable development.

20 Cf. LS p. 316, Inwood, op. cit., 282 n. 193 and cf. 179.

21 Cicero, *On Fate* 40, in an objection to the Stoic position which precedes Cicero's report of the Chrysippean cylinder-argument (n. 22). A. M. Ioppolo, 'Le cause antecedenti in Cicerone *De Fato* 40', in J. Barnes and M. Mignucci (eds), *Matter and Metaphysics*, Naples, Bibliopolis, 1989, 399–424, has suggested that the objection to which Chrysippus was responding was raised by Arcesilaus, and that Arcesilaus was objecting to the Stoic position as originally formulated by Zeno.

22 Cf. also Cicero, *On Fate* 41–5 (part in LS 62C), who has the contrast between the way in which a cylinder will roll and that in which a cone will. R. W. Sharples, *Cicero*, On Fate, *and Boethius*, Consolation of Philosophy *IV.5–7 and V*, Warminster, Aris and Phillips, 1991, 191.

23 Cicero, *On Fate* 30 = LS 55S; cf. Diogenianus cited by Eusebius, *Preparation of the Gospel* 6.8.25ff. = LS 62F; Origen, *Against Celsus* 2.20 = *SVF* 2.957. Cf. Sharples, op. cit., 92–5, 180–1.

24 Cf. Seneca, *On Providence* 4.5. Plutarch, *SR* 47 1057AB = LS 41F cites Chrysippus as saying that God produces false impressions but it is our fault if we assent to them.

25 Gilbert Ryle, *Dilemmas*, Cambridge, Cambridge University Press, 1954, ch. 2.

26 Cicero, *On Fate* 19, cf. 28.

27 R. Taylor, 'Determinism', in P. Edwards (ed.), *Encyclopedia of Philosophy*, New York, Macmillan/The Free Press, 1967, vol. 2, p. 369.

28 See for instance the criticisms in D. J. O'Connor, *Free Will*, London, Macmillan, 1972, ch. 11.

29 According to Cicero Carneades also spoke of chance events as exceptions to determinism; though the examples given could be accommodated in a determinist account, and from Cicero's account Carneades' view of the relation between chance events and choices seems at least unclear. Cf. P. L. Donini, *Ethos: Aristotele e il determinismo*, Alessandria (Torino), dell'Orso, 134–6.

30 A. A. Long, *Hellenistic Philosophy*, 2nd edn, London, Duckworth, 1986, 103–4.

5 HOW CAN I BE HAPPY?

1 A. W. H. Adkins, *Merit and Responsibility*, Oxford, Clarendon Press, 1960, 2.

2 K. J. Dover, *Greek Popular Morality*, Oxford, Basil Blackwell, 1974, 2–3 n. 3.

3 See n. 5 to Chapter One.

4 In a time before efficient artificial light the ancients began their evening meal in mid-afternoon and went to bed at dusk. Eating by lamplight was therefore a sign of extravagance and luxury. See Seneca, *Letter* 122.1–3. But Lucretius is also echoing Homer, *Odyssey* 7.100–2.

5 Literally 'care for their bodies'.
6 This identification of desires of the various types is controversial. It
  follows Annas 192–3 in giving credence to the scholion on *PD* 29 (=
  LS 21I), rather than to the anonymous commentary on Aristotle's
  Ethics (*Commentaria in Aristotelem Graeca* 20, p. 171.23–8 Heylbut =
  Usener, *Epicurea* 456), which gives desires for food and clothing as
  necessary, desire for sex as natural but non-necessary, and desire for
  specific types of the first two as unnatural – which last seems implausible as a general statement, though Annas points out, citing *PD* 30 =
  LS 21E, that a specific natural but non-necessary desire may become
  pathologically excessive and so unnatural. It seems unlikely that Epicurus would suppose that we have as much a need for sex as for clothing
  (Annas 193 n. 29); but that point is covered if both are necessary but
  the latter, though not the former, necessary for life itself.
7 By P. Boyancé, *Lucrèce et l'épicurisme*, Paris, Presses Universitaires de
  France, 1963, 260–2.
8 See on this also Annas 349.
9 J. S. Purinton, 'Epicurus on the *telos*', *Phronesis* 38 (1993), 281–320.
10 And, one might add, mortal creatures at least, though not the gods,
   are inevitably going to experience hunger and thirst and require replenishment throughout their lives. Purinton, indeed, does not want to
   restrict kinetic pleasures to those accompanying replenishment. If one
   does so it follows that Epicurus' gods cannot experience kinetic
   pleasures.
11 See on this Annas 86.
12 Nussbaum 212ff. Her whole discussion of the issue (192–238) is essential reading.
13 Purinton, op. cit., 317–18 n. 70, argues that the happy Epicurean can
   wish to prolong his or her life and hence to prolong (though not
   increase) his or her pleasure, while also holding that death is not an
   evil because, while it will deprive one of pleasure one would otherwise
   have had, one will not *miss* that pleasure. The last point, however,
   brings us back to the question whether the argument that death is no
   concern of ours once it has happened also shows that it should be
   no concern of ours now.
14 Cf., however, J. L. Moles, 'The Cynics and Politics', in André Laks
   and Malcolm Schofield (eds), *Justice and Generosity: Proceedings of
   the 6th Symposium Hellenisticum*, Cambridge, Cambridge University
   Press, 1995, 129–58.
15 M. Schofield, 'Two Stoic Approaches to Justice', in Laks and Schofield,
   op. cit., 196, has suggested that *oikeiôsis* might be rendered by 'identifying with'.
16 DL 7.109 = LS 59E. The actions, such as taking care of one's health,
   which are there described as appropriate 'without particular circumstances' must be, not ones that are appropriate *regardless* of the circumstances (for there are occasions when looking after one's health
   should not be one's overriding concern), but rather ones that are not
   appropriate *only* in special circumstances. (I am grateful to George
   Boys-Stones for clarifying this point to me.) There was debate among

members of the school over the usefulness of generalised precepts (Seneca, *Letters on Morals* 94–5; cf. Annas 96–108; Phillip Mitsis, 'Seneca on Reason, Rules and Moral Development', in J. Brunschwig and M. C. Nussbaum (eds), *Justice and Generosity*, Cambridge, Cambridge University Press, 1993, 285–312).

17 An example much older than Stoicism; Plutarch, *Life of Solon* 17.1, says that the seventh-century BC Athenian law code of Draco punished vegetable-thieves and temple-robbers equally; hence the expression 'Draconian'.

18 Cf. Annas 274.

19 Such a position is attributed to Polemo, the fourth head of Plato's Academy and Zeno's teacher, in Cicero, *On Ends* 4.51.

20 Although it is worth stressing, with Francesca Alesse, *Panezio di Rodi e la tradizione Stoica*, Naples, Bibliopolis, 1994, 250, that rejection of divination need not involve rejection of every form of interconnectedness in the universe – the former presupposes the latter, but not vice versa.

21 R. J. Hankinson, *The Sceptics*, London, Routledge, 1995, 305ff.; cf. Annas 362.

6 WHAT ABOUT OTHER PEOPLE?

1 So Hermarchus, Epicurus' successor as head of the school, cited by Porphyry, *On Abstinence* 1.7–9 = LS 22M. Hermarchus says 'laws' rather than 'legal sanctions'; presumably, even if everyone abided by the agreement, laws might still exist as the expression of its content, and what is necessitated by the fact that some people do not in fact abide by the agreement is the laws' provision of *penalties*. Perhaps, indeed, Hermarchus thinks of law itself in terms of the assignment of penalties.

2 Epicurus' associate Colotes, cited by Plutarch, *Against Colotes* 1124D = LS 22R; but see further p. 122.

3 V. Goldschmidt, 'La théorie épicurienne de la droit', in J. Barnes *et al.* (eds), *Science and Speculation*, Cambridge (see Suggestions for Further Reading), 1982, 304–26.

4 Probably including both men and women; at any rate women as well as men figure among Epicurus' correspondents. See Nussbaum 117.

5 'Virtue' (*aretê*) is the MS reading, 'choiceworthy' (*hairetê*) an emendation (not accepted by LS). But whichever reading we adopt, the point is that a contrast between pleasure as an instrumental good and as intrinsically good need not imply that the intrinsic goodness is not itself referred, in a different way indeed, to the individual's ultimate aim, pleasure.

6 For the sequel see pp. 85–6.

7 Cf. on this Annas 273-4.

8 Cf. M. Griffin, *Seneca: A Philosopher in Politics*, 2nd edn, Oxford, Clarendon Press, 1992, 365–6.

9 Both male and female, as with Plato's Rulers. See M. Schofield, *The*

Stoic Idea of the City, Cambridge, Cambridge University Press, 1991, 43–6; Nussbaum 322; and n. 12 to Chapter Two.

10 Schofield, op. cit., 110–11.

11 Schofield, op. cit., 100. Plutarch's subsequent statement (1076A = LS 61J) that Zeus and the sage benefit each other whenever they encounter a movement of the other might seem to provide a direct link between egoism and altruism; in benefiting others I benefit myself (so LS p. 377). But it is important to stress that the argument is confined to *sages*, and that the benefit in question must be true benefit which only the sage can receive – we are not concerned with cases like benefiting one's own soul by (e.g.) removing somebody else's poverty or sickness, for poverty is not an evil nor wealth a good. The benefit one sage derives from another must rather be interpreted, with Schofield, loc. cit., in terms of sharing in the virtue of the universe as a whole.

12 But for a more positive assessment of Cynic cosmopolitanism cf. J. L. Moles, 'The Cynics and Politics', in A. Laks and M. Schofield (eds), *Justice and Generosity*, Cambridge, Cambridge University Press, 1995, 129–58; above, Chapter Five, n. 14.

13 The notable exception being the statement of Alcidamas, 'God has set all free; nature has made no one a slave', cited by a scholion on Aristotle, *Rhetoric* 1373b18 (cf. W. K. C. Guthrie, *History of Greek Philosophy*, vol. 3, Cambridge, Cambridge University Press, 1969, 159 and n. 2).

14 He had risen from humble origins to become consul; but he is still, Horace jests, as much a barber as the Stoic sage is a king.

15 Bernard Williams, *Shame and Necessity*, Berkeley, University of California Press, 1993, 115–17.

16 See on this G. Watson, 'The Natural Law and Stoicism', in A. A. Long (ed.), *Problems in Stoicism*, London, Athlone Press, 1971, 216–38; Schofield, op. cit., 103.

7 EPILOGUE

1 The souls of the dead are described as spirits (*daimones*) once they have left the body; Sextus *M* 9.74. For spirits watching over mankind see also DL 7.151.

2 The quotation is from Virgil, *Aeneid* 8.353.

3 J. M. Rist, *Stoic Philosophy*, Cambridge, Cambridge University Press, 1969, 284.

4 Marcus means 'semen'; cf. *Meditations* 6.13. But the word he uses both here and there means literally 'nose-slime', 'snot'.

5 The word Marcus uses applies to embalmed bodies, and that is its literal meaning here; but it was also commonly used of meat or fish preserved by salting, drying or smoking.

6 I.e. Athens; Aristophanes, fr. 110 Edmonds.

7 Cf. Heraclitus, KRS 215.

SUGGESTIONS FOR
FURTHER READING

This list is highly selective; advice on further reading beyond that indicated here will be found in many of the books listed below.

TEXTS AND TRANSLATIONS

The standard collection of texts and translations is A. A. Long and D. N. Sedley, *The Hellenistic Philosophers*, Cambridge, Cambridge University Press, 1987. For Epicurus and his followers see also Brad Inwood and L. P. Gerson, introd. D. S. Hutchinson, *The Epicurus Reader*, Indianapolis, Hackett Publishing Co., 1994, and, for later Scepticism, Julia Annas and Jonathan Barnes, *Sextus Empiricus: Outlines of Scepticism*, Cambridge, Cambridge University Press, 1994. Translations of the authors of the Roman period (Cicero, Lucretius, Seneca, Epictetus, Marcus Aurelius, Diogenes Laertius) may be found in the Loeb Classical Library and in many cases also in the Penguin Classics series; note also John M. Cooper and J. F. Procopé (eds), *Seneca, Moral and Political Essays* (Cambridge Texts in the History of Political Thought), Cambridge, Cambridge University Press, 1995, and C. Gill and R. Hard, *Epictetus, The Discourses, the Handbook, fragments*, London, Everyman (J. M. Dent), 1995. The inscription of Diogenes of Oenoanda is cited from the new edition, with English translation, by Martin Ferguson Smith, *Diogenes of Oenoanda: The Epicurean Inscription*, Naples, Bibliopolis, 1993.

GENERAL BOOKS ON HELLENISTIC PHILOSOPHY

A. A. Long, *Hellenistic Philosophy*, London, Duckworth, ²1986.

On the Roman period:
J. G. F. Powell (ed.), *Cicero the Philosopher*, Oxford, Clarendon Press, 1995.
M. Griffin and J. Barnes (eds.), *Philosophia Togata*, Oxford, Clarendon Press, 1989.

On particular aspects:

Julia Annas, *Hellenistic Philosophy of Mind*, Berkeley, University of California Press, 1992.

Julia Annas, *The Morality of Happiness*, New York, Oxford University Press USA, 1993.

Martha C. Nussbaum, *The Therapy of Desire: Theory and Practice in Hellenistic Ethics*, Princeton, Princeton University Press, 1994.

The proceedings of the successive Symposia Hellenistica:

M. Schofield *et al.* (eds.), *Doubt and Dogmatism*, Oxford, Clarendon Press, 1980.

J. Barnes *et al.* (eds.), *Science and Speculation*, Cambridge, Cambridge University Press, and Paris, Maison des Sciences de l'Homme, 1982.

M. Schofield and G. Striker (eds.), *The Norms of Nature*, Cambridge, Cambridge University Press, and Paris, Maison des Sciences de l'Homme, 1986.

J. Barnes and M. Mignucci (eds), *Matter and Metaphysics*, Naples, Bibliopolis, 1988.

J. Brunschwig and M. C. Nussbaum (eds.), *Passions and Perceptions*, Cambridge, Cambridge University Press, 1993.

A. Laks and M. Schofield (eds), *Justice and Generosity*, Cambridge, Cambridge University Press, 1995.

The collections of essays in the series Companions to Ancient Thought, *edited by Stephen Everson (Cambridge, Cambridge University Press)*: 1, *Epistemology*, 1990; 2, *Psychology*, 1991; 3, *Language*, 1994.

EPICUREANISM

J. M. Rist, *Epicurus: An Introduction*, Cambridge, Cambridge University Press, 1972.

P. Mitsis, *Epicurus' Ethical Theory*, Ithaca, Cornell University Press, 1988.

Particularly helpful for the understanding of Lucretius is:

D. West, *The Imagery and Poetry of Lucretius*, Edinburgh, Edinburgh University Press, 1969.

For the subsequent influence of Epicureanism:

Howard Jones, *The Epicurean Tradition*, London, Routledge, 1989.

STOICISM

J. M. Rist, *Stoic Philosophy*, Cambridge, Cambridge University Press, 1969.

A. A. Long (ed.), *Problems in Stoicism*, London, Athlone Press, 1971.

F. H. Sandbach, *The Stoics*, London, Chatto and Windus, 1975.

B. Inwood, *Ethics and Human Action in Early Stoicism*, Oxford, Clarendon Press, 1986.

SCEPTICISM

C. L. Stough, *Greek Scepticism*, Berkeley, University of California Press, 1969.

J. Annas and J. Barnes, *The Modes of Scepticism*, Cambridge, Cambridge University Press, 1985.

Harold Tarrant, *Scepticism or Platonism?*, Cambridge, Cambridge University Press, 1985.

R. J. Hankinson, *The Sceptics* (The Arguments of the Philosophers series), London, Routledge, 1995.

INDEX

149

physics, 33–43; politics, 7, 134;
    epistemology 11–32
equilibrium (*isonomia*) 14, 65
equipollence 30
ethics 2–4, 82–4; Epicurean 82–99,
    116–23; Sceptic 113–15; Stoic
    82–4,100–12, 123–7
eudaimonia see happiness
Eudemus 24
eupatheiai 70
Euripides 22, 54, 71
evil, problem of 53–5

fate 49–53, 74–6
fear 68–70, 133; *see also* anxiety;
    death, fear of; heavenly
    phenomena, fear of
feelings *see* emotions, passions
fire 45, 48
Fitzgerald, Edward 2
form and matter 35
fourth, unnamed type of atoms in
    soul 62–4, 66
Frede, Michael 24
free choice, free will 64–6, 72,
    79–81
freedom, in Stoicism 76–8; *see also*
    freedom from anxiety
friendship 87, 118–20, 122–4
Furley, David 65
future: asymmetry of past and
    future 95; truth concerning
    future 78–9

Galen 72
Galileo 42
genera, in Stoicism *see* categories
goal *see* purpose of life
god, gods 14, 131; divine element
    in each individual 128–9, 132; in
    Epicurus 14, 18–19, 56–8, 95; in
    Stoicism 21, 48, 74–5; *see also*
    principle, active; Zeus
Goldschmidt, Victor 117
Goodness 21, 83–4
goods, bodily and external, and
    happiness 100, 109–10
Griffin, Miriam 124

Hankinson, Jim 31–2, 114
happiness 83–4, 87, 99, 100–1,
    108–9, 116
head 60, 67
health 102, 110
heavenly phenomena, Epicurus on
    knowledge of 14–15; fear of, 93
Hecaton 124
Hellenistic philosophy, modern
    attitudes to 2–3
Heraclitus 45, 67, 125
Herculaneum, Herculaneum
    papyri 6–7
Hermarchus 144
Hesiod 5
hexis 45
Hierocles 123
Hippias 125
Homer 131
Horace 1–2, 95, 97, 106, 126, 129
human insignificance 130–2

images (*eidôla*) 12–13, 18–19
immortality *see* death, survival
    after
impulse 69, 73–5
incorporeals, in Stoicism 47
indifferents 102
individuals 28
individuals: and universals 47–8;
    differences between 28; divine
    element in 128–9, 132; part of
    greater whole 67, 111–13,
    128–30, 132
indivisible minima 36–7, 39
infinity of space and time, in
    atomists 14
instinct 101, 105
intellectualism 72
intermediate propositions 47
Inwood, Brad 70
isonomia see equilibrium

joy 70
judgement *see* reason
Julius Caesar 7
justice 116–18
Juvenal 72